"ALL HIS RIGHTS"

by

G.C. FLOYD

Copyright © G. C. Floyd

ISBN 0 9533836 0 1

A CIP catalogue record for this book is obtainable from the British Library.

Typeset and printed by West Somerset Free Press, 5 Long Street, Williton, Taunton, Somerset TA4 4QN.

Published by the author

The moral right of the author has been asserted.

DISCLAIMER
Every possible effort has been made to contact copyright holders of photographs reproduced in this work. The author can entertain no claim from any person after publication.

All photographs are by kind permission of the artists concerned.

FOREWORD

My only qualification to write on Exmoor's deer is to have been born in an isolated woodland cottage and been able to follow the deer tracks since I was a small boy, first with my father, and this interest in our fellow creatures has and continues to stay with me. I am short of formal educational qualifications but hope that my enthusiasm for my subject and my local practical lessons in woodcraft, coupled with the thousands of happy hours I have spent in the field, will stand me in good stead as I make this attempt to write this study and try to share with you the joy this animal has brought to my life in this my book of wild Red deer "All His Rights".

ILLUSTRATIONS

The black and white photographs and colour plates in this book were all taken by the Author.

They are all shots of true Wild Deer on Exmoor.

None of the photographs were taken in deer parks or sanctuaries

To

My late Father,

Charles Gordon Floyd

Dad, a great countryman who loved Exmoor.

INDEX

PAGE

1	Introduction
3	Description of Exmoor's deer
11	Deer watching and photography
29	Deer numbers and distribution
31	Hinds and calving
35	The Deer's food
39	The rut
45	Antlers
48	Antler renewal
54	Antler development
59	Deer control on Exmoor
62	Hunting of deer on Exmoor
73	Deer shooting on Exmoor
76	Stag horning
81	Some favourite stags
95	Conclusion

ACKNOWLEDGEMENTS

I am indebted to Mr. Mark Blathwayt (A.R.I.C.S.), for allowing me to reside in his cottage over the years on the "Porlock Manor Estate" and for the freedom I have enjoyed on his estate enabling me to study the deer.

Thanks also to the estate staff, I am most grateful to the officers and staff of "The Exmoor National Park Authority", "The National Trust" and "The League Against Cruel Sports".

REFERENCES

BATESON, P (1997)   The behavioural and physiological effects of culling red deer. Report to the council of The National Trust.

LANGBEIN, J (1997)   The ranging behaviour, habitat use and impact of deer in oak woods and heather moors of Exmoor and the Quantock Hills.

LLOYD, E.R. (1970)   The wild red deer of Exmoor, Exmoor Press, Dulverton

LLOYD, E.R. (1975)   The wild red deer of Exmoor, Exmoor Press, Dulverton, Second Edition

MACDERMOT, E.T (1936)   The Devon and Somerset Staghounds (1907 - 1936) London; Collins

GOSS, F (1931)   Memoirs of a stag harbourer, London; H.F. and G. Witherby.

"ALL HIS RIGHTS"

by

G.C. FLOYD

A STUDY OF THE WILD RED DEER OF EXMOOR

Wild Red deer on Exmoor

ALL HIS RIGHTS

by G.C.FLOYD

INTRODUCTION

Mention deer and Exmoor to anyone and it can conjure up varying reactions, some of them highly emotive depending on where the person lives and what they do and their opinions on country sports. For those fortunate enough to have seen deer at first hand on Exmoor, both residents and visitors, for most of them it is the happy recollection of these sightings. The elegance and the nobleness of this creature is something people remember. To some it is the excitement of watching and following hounds hunting this large elusive quarry and to others it is the fight to abolish blood sports. To the farmer and landowner, the reaction can be sheer anger, as they survey their damaged crops and trees. A few will be involved professionally in deer management with the rifle. Other self-appointed shooters look to deer for financial gain and their desire is to persuade landowners to allow them to shoot deer. For the opportunist, small time poacher, it is how to do it without permission. Whatever the reaction, the majority are interested in the welfare of the species.

The predominant species of deer on Exmoor is the Red deer and the West Country is the last main English stronghold for this, Britain's largest surviving wild animal. Very little study has been done on the animal, mainly due to the amount of woodcraft necessary to carry out a detailed study. It has been my privilege as a native Exmoor man to have spent much of my life in the field recording and studying and photographing Exmoor's deer. I write with a deep respect and love for the animal. As the stag's head is the emblem of Exmoor, proper management and fair treatment for deer seems of utmost importance. I hope the following work will do something for their welfare.

DESCRIPTION OF EXMOOR'S DEER

There are 40 or so species of deer in the world, many of these species are today in danger of extinction. Britain has two surviving native species, the Red and the Roe deer, and both today are found on Exmoor. From time to time throughout history, deer from other parts of the world have been introduced to our shores.

The best known of these species is the Fallow deer which has a long history in Britain. It is often said that this species was introduced to Britain by the Romans although there is archaeological evidence to suggest, a race of Fallow far more previous than this. Fallow deer were the principal species used for stocking deer parks as they thrive in captivity and also in the wild. Many escaped from these parks over the years to form wild herds in various parts of the country. The main concentration of fallow deer on Exmoor are found around the north eastern corner of the National Park.

Other introduced species of deer to Britain are the Asian Reeves Muntjac, Sika deer and the Chinese Water deer which today are found living wild in many parts of the country but are not found on Exmoor. Many people, probably in a bid to be the first, have claimed to have seen the Asian Reeves Muntjac deer on Exmoor. It is possible that like the Roe deer the Muntjac may turn up and achieve a successful establishment. Reports of sightings of this tiny deer are probably mistaken with Roe deer and as yet, there is no proof of this species' existence on Exmoor.

Sika or Japanese deer are approximately the same size as Fallow deer and were also introduced to deer parks in Britain. Later some were to escape to form independent wild herds in parts of the country. On Exmoor, Sika deer were once kept under park conditions at Pixton Park near Dulverton. Some escaped and for some time were known to be living in the Bray valley and Knowstone coverts south of the Exmoor National Park. The species has not been recorded for many years now and it is almost certain that they have died out. Of all the British deer, only the Sika deer and Red deer are of the same genus and can inter-breed. A Sika stag, if not able to find mates of his own species will rut with red deer hinds. The progeny is an inferior sized deer of red deer appearance. This almost certainly did happen in this part of the West Country for I have heard deer described from this area by locals as being the Bray valley dwarfs.

Chinese Water Deer have never been known on Exmoor and

because of the distance from the nearest population the chance is highly unlikely of this species making a natural establishment.

The following is a description of the three species of deer to be found on Exmoor.

Red Deer (Cervus Elaphus)

Red deer are the predominant species of deer on Exmoor and the largest surviving land mammal in Britain. The male Red deer is called a stag and female a hind. The young which are born in mid-summer are called calves. At maturity, a stag measures approximately 44 ins. at the shoulder and the hind 38 ins. Only the stag grows antlers which are shed annually in the spring and are regrown by the end of summer. As the stag matures, he grows larger and more complex antlers every year, until when he reaches old age, this is reversed and his head of antlers deteriorates every year which is known as "going back". Throughout the summer months, the stag's growing antlers are covered in a skin called velvet, which is grey in colour and like velvet to the touch.

Like all deer species, the Red deer's seasonal changes involve changes of the coat and its colour. The actual variation of appearance between individual Red deer is not so apparent as in say, the species Fallow deer. Difference between individual Red deers appearance is most noticeable in autumn and spring when coats are at various stages of this seasonal change.

During summer the stags and hinds wear a splendid coat of russet red and are in peak condition and look at their best. Between individuals this can vary from dark red to brown to a buff-coloured coat. The deer have light rump breeches and a short tufted tail which is called the flag. A prominent line of darker hair is found growing down some individuals backs. The new born calf's appearance is one of dark brown and covered with large light spots. At eight weeks old the spots have almost faded away as the calf loses his woolly baby coat for the normal Red deer coat.

As winter approaches the Red deer's coats darken with the autumn foliage. Autumn is the mating time for the Red deer which is known as the "rut". Prior to this the stags' neck hairs grow long to cover the swelling of the vocal region and to give them an impressive appearance.

The Red deer's winter coat is rough and thick and generally the stags are darker than the hinds. The winter coat can vary between

Stag in summer

Hind in summer

individuals from dark to light brown to even a gingery orange. The majority of hinds' coats lighten to a slate-grey. It is during winter that the deer's rump breeches are creamy white and most prominent.

During early May the Red deer's coats moult. For a while they appear extremely shabby with often noticeable bare patches. Clumps of the shed hair can be found anywhere in the country frequented by the deer.

The occurrence of an albino Red deer is extremely rare and I have only ever seen one true albino Red deer on Exmoor which was a young stag in the Molland Common district. Deer with patches of white hair on the body, though still a rarity, occur more often. For several years on the Quantock Hills there lived a white hind, though not a true albino, she was almost totally white. A few Red deer, especially old hinds and some stags, have prominent mealy-grey muscles.

The Red deer are gregarious but the constitution of the herds changes with the time of the year. For the most part of the year, generally stags and hinds live separate lives, living in their respective herds. The autumn is the mating time which is known as the "rut".

During September, stags become restless within their herds, affected by a gradual rising of the testosterone level, the male sexual hormone. By the beginning of October, all stags have left their home range areas and travelled away in search of the company of hinds. The rut is at a peak around mid-October and competition amongst stags is intense as each stag challenges and competes for possession of a hind herd.

Of the Red deer's vocabulary it is the sound of the challenge of the stag that is best known. On Exmoor this eerie sound is known as "balving" or "roaring". The sound somewhat resembles the bellow of a bull but with deeper intonation. The other common Red deer sound is barking, both stags and hinds will emit this warning call when they are nervous or suspicious of something or if they are surprised. Hinds bark a great deal more than stags especially during summer when they are nervous for their offspring. The newborn calf is generally silent except if it should be molested when it will emit a loud high-pitched bleat.

NOTE: One point of description, found to be fairly unique to the Red deer of Exmoor is the extremely prominent black rims to their ears, which is noticeable in the majority of individuals.

Roe Deer (Capreolus Capreolus)

Together with the Red deer, Roe are also native to the shores of the British Isles. The male Roe is called a buck and the female Roe is called a doe. The young which are born in June while dependent on their mothers are called kids. In comparison to the Red deer, the Roe is tiny. A full-grown buck at three years old measures about 26ins. at the shoulder while the doe is a couple of inches smaller. The buck carries short antlers which rarely exceed nine inches in length, and at maturity, normally have three tines from each antler. Quite the opposite to most other temperate species of deer, the buck sheds his antlers in autumn and these are regrown again by the spring.

The Roe is an extremely elegant little animal. They have long slender necks and dark lustrous eyes. The jet black nose is set off by one or sometimes two, white chin patches. The coat is changed twice a year. In winter, the Roe appear rabbit-grey with a large conspicuous white rump patch which is known as the target. In summer, they are a rich golden fox-red in various shades. The target is then yellowish or even orange in summer. The buck's target is smaller than that of the doe. The newborn kids are reddish in colour and are spotted with white. The spots are in lines along their bodies and disappear by the autumn.

Although Roe do form into small winter groups, unlike the Red deer, Roe cannot be described as gregarious. Generally bucks lead a solitary existence and the doe remains on her own with her offspring. The Roe rut falls between the 20th July and the 20th August. A buck takes up a rutting stand or territory and will strive to remain occupied in this area until the end of the rut. A buck's choice of territory that he takes up, is determined by the presence of the doe. The buck is signalled to the heat of the doe which lasts for three to four days by her scent and her call. Bucks will drive a doe till she will stand. Whilst they are driving, Roe frequently run in a circle or figure of eight. The same track is used time after time which is known as the "ring".

The most remarkable feature of the breeding cycle of Roe is that the embryos do not begin to develop in the wombs before December and this is known as delayed implantation, from which the doe will give birth about the second half of June. One or two kids are normally dropped, and on a rare occasion, three.

Roe deer are more vocal than most species of deer. The deer have a repertoire of barking alarms when they have seen or heard

Roe buck in an Exmoor Woodland

The Fallow deer

something they do not understand. This alarm call varies considerably between individuals depending on the age and the sex of the giver of the call. Fully mature bucks have a fighting bark which is given singly at intervals and is heard when two fully-grown bucks take up their stand fairly close together, or when one buck strays into another buck's territory.

The doe has a whistling mating call which she uses during the rut to signify her heat to a buck. This is another call where the pitch alters with the age of the animal. Does and kids also use a similar whistle to call each other.

Fallow Deer

It is generally accepted that Fallow deer are not native to the British Isles, although some archaeological remains have been found in deposits dating back to the ice age which does suggest a previous race. It is probable that they were introduced or reintroduced by the Romans, their origins being Asia Minor, Macedonia and the shores of the Mediterranean. Because Fallow deer thrive in captivity, they have always been the principal species for deer parks. They were certainly numerous at the time of the Normans who highly regarded this deer as a beast of the chase. Many parks were destroyed by Oliver Cromwell and escapees resulted and in this century, the necessity for food production during the two World Wars meant that parks were turned over to farming and many deer escaped.

Such is the origin of the wild Fallow deer that are found within the Exmoor National Park. With the disbandment of Dunster Deer Park and Nettlecombe Court some deer escaped and formed wild herds mainly in the large fir plantations centred around Croydon Hill. Generally it is only in this county in the North Eastern corner of Exmoor where wild Fallow are to be found.

Fallow deer are smaller than Red deer yet much larger than Roe deer. The male Fallow is called a buck and the female a doe, and the young are called fawns. The majority of Fallow fawns are born in the second week in June. Only the buck grows antlers and when adult at seven to eight years old, the buck's antlers are broadly palmated at the top. No other British deer carries antlers at all similar to Fallow. Like the stag the Fallow buck sheds his antlers in the spring and by late July, beginning of August a new pair are complete.

The Fallow deer's main characteristics are the variation between individuals and their distinctive tail which, at nine inches long, is longer than any other British deer. Fallow deer appear in four main colour varieties which are: brown (common), black, white or spotted. The summer and winter coat of each variety also differs with regular pattern. Fallow deer retain spots throughout their lives and in summer and winter it is with the spotted variety that these are most obvious. The black strain are said to have been imported from Scandinavia. In some areas it is the black strain of wild Fallow that predominates, as over years of hunting by predators and latterly by man, the black deer have been less conspicuous and have had the best chance of survival.

Like the Red deer, Fallow are gregarious and have a similar pattern of seasonal activity. For the most part of the year, bucks and does are set in their separate herds. Fallow bucks cast their antlers a few weeks later than Red deer stags, beginning with the older bucks that shed before the end of April, and then shedding continues throughout May.

After an autumn rut the gestation period for a Fallow doe like the Red deer hind, is eight months with no delayed implantation as with Roe deer. Single fawns are the rule, the occurrence of twins being very rare.

Competition amongst the Fallow bucks during the rut is intense. A master buck takes up his rutting stand and strives to defend his mastership throughout the peak of the rut, during mid October. Generally a rutting Fallow buck is far more vicious and violent than a Red deer stag. For the rut, the Fallow buck's neck hairs grow long and cover the swelling of the Adam's Apple. The sound of the challenge of a rutting Fallow buck is described as a groan and it is a grunting belching sound.

When communicating with each other, does and fawns make a low whickering note which the doe also makes in the company of the master buck on the rutting stand. Both bucks and does will occasionally emit a short deep bark when they are nervous and unsure of something or when they are surprised.

There is no Fallow deer hunting with hounds on Exmoor and generally they are shot by Forestry Commission marksmen and by landowners when the deer roam onto agricultural land.

DEER WATCHING AND PHOTOGRAPHY

Watching and studying deer is an absorbing and inexpensive hobby. One essential piece of equipment is a pair of binoculars or a monocular or telescope. It is a mistake to buy high-powered magnification for deer watching as with the magnification of the object comes magnification of any unsteadiness on the part of the user. Also the field of view is reduced making any necessary quick focusing difficult and time consuming. My personal preference is a good quality pair of 8.30 binoculars which are small and light for carrying and have a sharp image in the commonplace low light conditions confronted with when watching wild deer. With lower magnification, there is less demand on the lens and they are a far better proposition.

As their main enemy, wild deer understandably are fearing and timid towards human beings and to be able to get consistently close to the deer for observation or photography, requires skills of wood craft, knowledge of the animal, an ability to track and read the signs of deer, an intimate knowledge of the country they inhabit and, most of all, a respect and appreciation of the senses the species has had to develop for survival.

Deer possess four main senses with which they perceive their environment. These are sight, hearing, smell and touch. Any slight sound or scent or movement will alert the deer and bring these senses into full play. The head is lifted with the eyes and large erect ears pinpointed at the point of suspicion with a moist nose twitching and sampling the air. The slightest mistake by the most cautious and skilful of stalkers can cause this alarm and inevitably the hasty departure of the deer. Yet in the world the deer live in, the deer become well-accustomed to the sights and sounds and scents that do them no harm. On Exmoor, the Red deer will noticeably ignore the regular comings and goings of low-flying aeroplanes, people walking and riding on the regular paths, also cars on the road and farm vehicles about their work on the land. A car is probably the best 'hide' and observation point for deer watching one can have.

For deer photography, good equipment is important but just as important is the individual's commitment to the task of getting close to the deer and a steady hand enabling one to hand-hold and not have the burden of the weight and bulk of tripods, of which one rarely has the time or opportunity to set up. My favourite combination is a 35mm. SLR camera with a 500mm lens using a

400ASA fast film. Speed and efficiency of use of one's equipment is vital and so you must know your equipment inside out and be able to use it as if it was an extension of yourself.

It is the landowner who owns the wild deer and if one desires to go and photograph, then permission must be sought before you begin. Even with permission there are still rules and ethics to heed. At all times one should put the interest of the deer and their welfare before one's desire to get pictures. If an attempt to stalk deer is made, whether successful or not, once the deer are alert and aware of your presence in their home then that is the time to leave as carefully as one approached them. The most satisfying feeling is being able to stalk wild deer, take a photograph and leave without them knowing you have been there.

Once the art of spying deer before they see you has been mastered, then one can begin to enjoy the pleasure of stalking wild deer. A plan of approach must be worked out and the first thing and most important is to consider the direction of the wind. The deer's sense of smell is most acute and as well as scenting danger, they can also follow each other and other animals just by smell. The deer are regularly licking and keeping their nose moist and alert. At all times, one must endeavour to approach deer with the wind blowing from them to you. One sniff of what is to them, the poisonous aroma of man, will soon send them fleeing. As well as when planning an approach to deer you have spied, it will also often reap reward when just out searching for deer to remember, for example in a woodland, to walk into the wind. When one is not blessed with the advantage of a strong wind for stalking and when one's quarry is, as they often are, in a steep valley side, then one will obviously encounter the difficulty of swirling wind direction, which at times can be unpredictable and impossible to judge.

As acute as the deer's sense of smell is, likewise is their sense of hearing. The deer have large ears which can pick up the slightest sound from considerable distances. Obviously it is advantageous to stalk alone. Avoid clothes that rustle, especially waterproofs and beware of rattling keys and loose change in pockets. The best footwear would be none at all, so do not choose heavy footwear, like hob nail boots and beware of looseness and flapping straps. Learning to walk cautiously and silently, avoiding dry leaves and snapping twigs, combined with the concentration of the spying of the deer, is somewhat of an art in itself.

The deer's eyesight is the easiest of the three main senses of the deer to fool. Consistent with herbivores, deer probably are colour blind and though quick to detect the slightest movement, if one is well-camouflaged with the surroundings and remains frozen when the deer are looking, one can remain undetected from surprisingly close-range. Covering one's hands and face in comfort will also cut down incidences of being detected by the deer's eyesight.

It is in the last few yards of a stalk when all one's skill, precision and a certain amount of good fortune, has got you right beside this elusive wild animal. Adrenalin will be running high and it can be extremely exhilarating. At times, one dare not breathe or move a muscle, especially when suddenly rendered frozen by one deer's sign of slight suspicion. With patience and luck, and probably cramp, the deer's suspicion will pass, to give one the opportunity to once again inch one's way even closer or settle for the position one has achieved. With experience one will instinctively know when to start to prepare to shoot. One will also know when the situation requires a slight noise to alert the deer and make your picture. Avoid whistling as this is a noise the deer immediately associate with human beings. To take full advantage of the deer's inquisitive nature, I have found that a quiet mimic of a sheep will cause the deer to stop and look and wonder where the sheep is. On occasions, they can become so inquisitive that they will come in closer to investigate.

Just occasionally, one can surprise a deer into freezing with indecision. I well recall such an incident I experienced with a lone stag that was just shedding the velvet. Conditions were perfect and I had stalked him to 10 metres. Eventually I was forced to give away my presence with a noise. Instead of rushing away he stood and looked at me in amazement, as if in a state of shock that I was there. *(See illustration next page).* He licked his nose several times as if he was confused as to why his most acute form of defence, his smell, had let him down. After a while my reaction was to gently talk to him as this has a relaxing effect on the deer. With that he slowly moved away.

For every successful close encounter with deer while stalking, one will have many more unsuccessful attempts. At times, one could be led to think that the deer possess an extra-perceptionary sense. The woods and moors are their home and the slightest sign of change will make them nervous and uneasy. Calls of other animals, especially alarm calls of birds and the sudden movement of other creatures can be enough to cause the deer to leave the scene long before you have arrived. Lone deer are obviously easier to stalk than

a large herd and in the case of the stags, one does have a pair of antlers which act as an extra guide when you are stalking the deer.

From a lifetime of hunting and stalking deer for the camera on Exmoor, one particular photograph I achieved and the stalk I did to get it, stands out in my memory the most. An extremely wild and wary big stag was rutting in the district. On two previous occasions my attempts to photograph him had failed.

It was a foggy, damp autumn morning. After much searching I had failed to locate the old stag

He stood and looked at me in amazement.

and returning up the valley, I paused for a last scan with the binoculars. Suddenly, I saw his antlers move in a big patch of bracken where he was hiding in the shelter of a small combe. With heart lifted and a check of the wind, I set about a long detour before I could make an approach. Unfortunately as he was lying in the middle of the bracken patch, getting really close was extremely difficult as the bracken was thick and brittle and hard to crawl silently across. I could see the tops of his antlers ahead of me, but I was stumped as to how to get any closer. For a while I lay there trying to work out a solution. Suddenly almost like an answer to a prayer, a violent sudden moorland hail storm swept across the path of me and the deer. It only lasted for probably about a minute, but throughout its duration I swiftly moved forward, my sound masked by the violence of the storm.

The storm had abated and although I was in a great position, my next problem was drying and demisting the camera lens. The tension was becoming unbearable, so I plucked up the courage to slowly rise from the bracken. He detected my presence immediately and there was just a couple of seconds to take a shot *(see below)*. In no time he was climbing out of the next valley, followed by a hind and calf that I had not known were there. They paused to look back, then disappeared into the mist. Though soaking wet and facing a long walk home, I was more than happy with the outcome of that memorable stalk.

There was just a couple of seconds to take a shot

DEER NUMBERS AND DISTRIBUTION

The principal home of the wild Red deer of the West Country of England is within the confines of the Exmoor National Park boundary where one finds an abundance of suitable wild habitat for deer in the woods and moors of this area. As seen from the description of Exmoor's Deer, the Red deer share this home with the less common Roe and Fallow deer. The deer's Exmoor home is a patchwork of high grass moor and heather moor. Steep wooded valleys and farmland interwoven with numerous roads and small villages, Exmoor boasts some of the finest countryside scenery in England.

As an original woodland animal, the deer make full use of its availability on Exmoor. Approximately half of the wild Red deer harbour in the covers afforded in the main valleys of Horner, the Exe and the Barle. In favoured areas the deer can be observed regularly at any time of the day throughout the Exmoor year, while in another area the sight of a Red deer can be extremely rare, such is the way of the distribution of Red deer on Exmoor.

The Exmoor National Park has no high deer-proof fence to confine the Red deer and so they heed no boundaries. For many years, there has been a separate sizeable population of wild Red deer on the Quantock Hills to the East of Exmoor. The Quantock Red deer are today self-contained and somewhat marooned from Exmoor with the

Exmoor Country

modern development of the country between the two areas and I would say there was little, if any interaction between these areas today.

Good numbers of deer harbour immediately south of Exmoor and of these, there is regular interaction across the National Park boundary. Further south, beyond the old Barnstaple / Taunton railway line, wild Red deer are found. This area is known as the Tiverton country and it is the country that the Tiverton Stag hounds hunt. The Chulmleigh and Cheldon covers are strongholds for the Red deer in this district. To the west of the National Park, the covers around Arlington and the country down to Barnstaple hold fair numbers of Red deer.

On the more distant fringes, small numbers of Red deer have re-established themselves on Dartmoor, returning to an old stronghold as well as Red deer being reported in the woodlands around Bodmin Moor and right down into Cornwall. Occasionally the odd wild Red deer has been seen on Haldon Hill near Exeter, and the occasional Red stag has sought the company of the Fallow deer in Powderham Park on the Exe estuary.

Estimations of numbers of the wild Red deer within the Exmoor National Park at best, can only really be a well-informed guess and always open for dispute. The deer are woodland animals. Stags especially have a large range, moving throughout the year according to the season and food availability. In 1936, E.T. MacDermot thought that Red deer numbers had dropped to about six hundred, and although there was considerable disturbance on Exmoor during World War 2, Dick Lloyd in his "Wild Red Deer of Exmoor" in 1970, estimated that there were between five and seven hundred. In the 1975 edition, he revised the figure upwards to between six and eight hundred. The Exmoor Natural History Society's assessment for 1987 was about eight hundred with a further two hundred immediately south of the National Park boundary.

To personally assess the number of Exmoor wild Red deer, I have divided the National Park into seventeen areas. For each area I describe what the deer situation has been during the time of my study of the animal and give an estimation of the numbers today. The hind herd estimations obviously include calves and young males. Stag herd estimations most importantly include how many are observed to be in their prime with full antler potential. Finally I break down the numbers to assess the quality and balance of the sexes of the Red deer on Exmoor.

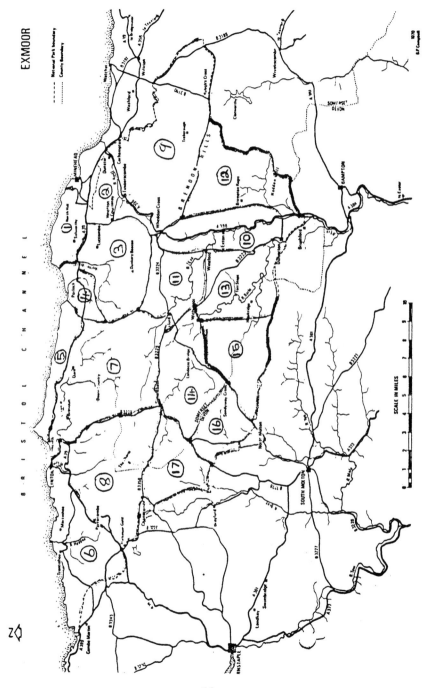

KEY TO NUMBERED AREAS

1. North Hill, Minehead - Selworthy / Bossington Woods

2. Grabbist Hill, Dunster to Wheddon Cross, down to Wootton Courtenay

3. Dunkery Area from Brockwell to Lucott Cross (Horner Woods)

4. Hawkcombe Valley, Porlock Common, Porlock Parks / Worthy Wood

5. Coastal Area, Worthy Toll Road to Foreland Point

6. All west of Lynmouth, north of the A39 to Blackmoor Gate to National Park boundary.

7. Forest of Exmoor or Parish of Simonsbath. Area between Simonsbath to Lynmouth, to Hawkcombe Head.

8. All west of Lynmouth B3223 to Simonsbath to National Park boundary in west.

9. East of A396 to Wheddon Cross, north of Brendon Hill Ridge Road, Dunster, Croydon Hill, Treborough and Monksilver

10. Quarme and Exe Valley on either side of A396

11. South of Wheddon Cross to Exford, Great Staddon & Exe Valley

12. South of the Brendon Hill Ridge Road to National Park boundary, Brompton Regis, Haddon

13. The Barle Valley, Withypool to Dulverton and the Danesbrook

14. Barle Valley, Simonsbath to Withypool

15. Withypool Hill to Molland Common to Twitchen

16. South of Fyldon Ridge to Heasely Mill

17. All south of Challacombe-Simonsbath Road to Bray

EXMOOR 1995
DEER NUMBERS AND DISTRIBUTION

Area 1, North Hill, Minehead, Selworthy / Bossington Woods

This area of outstanding natural beauty offers excellent habitat for the deer with a wild and remote coastal stretch, heathland and an abundance of deciduous cover. From all accounts, it seems clear that the Red deer's heyday in this area, was around the turn of the century and during the war years, the Red deer taking advantage of the increase in woodland cover that was planted by the then owners, the Acland family, who in time gave their land to the National Trust. Red deer numbers gradually declined and during the 1960's there were almost no Red deer on this side of the A39 from Porlock to Minehead. During the early 1970's, the deer began to return, gradually re-establishing themselves.

Of recent years, although numbers have never been plentiful, it is all the more rewarding to see them. The area has produced some fine big stags, a few travelling across to the Horner district for the rut. Today, the Red deer in the area are harbouring more on the cliffs and in the country close to Minehead. I have had good recent sightings of Red and Roe deer. I saw eight stags in Bramble Combe on the cliffs in the winter of 1987 and overall the wild Red deer

Area 1 North Hill. This area has produced some fine big stags.

appear to be faring very well in this area.
(Estimation of numbers: Red deer 40, ie. 30 hind herd, 10 stag herd (4 mature).

Area 2, Grabbist Hill, Dunster to Headon Cross, down to Wootton Courtenay

This is a large woodland area consisting of mainly commercial forestry with some deciduous woodland and open common land. The area was once famous for its stags producing some of the heaviest deer recorded on Exmoor. Since I have known the area, it has suffered a steady decline and today the Grabbist stag is quite a rarity with few achieving any size or antler growth of note. The surviving Red deer population consists of mainly hinds. Alcombe Common is a reliable place to watch them. Some of the deer have become unpopular recently in the winter months when they have been able to easily get into the allotments at Dunster. Roe deer also can be found in this area.

(Estimation of numbers: Red deer 80, ie. 74 hind herd, 6 stag herd (2 mature).

Area 3, Dunkery Area from Brockwell to Lucott Cross (Horner Woods)

Most of this area is owned by the National Trust and part of the Holnicote estate. The scenery is the best Exmoor has to offer with the largest remaining areas of heather moor around Dunkery Beacon at 1705 feet, the highest point on Exmoor. From up on the moor, one can see into the large wooded valley of Horner and down to the Vale of Porlock. This area is also the heart of Exmoor deer country with the largest surviving concentrations today. As well as the Red, a few Roe deer are found in the area as well.

The Red deer have probably always lived in this area since earliest times and good numbers are still there today. During my study, numbers have remained fairly stable. Traditionally most of the area is hind country and a rutting stronghold for the stags that move onto the moor during the autumn. Despite numbers remaining fairly stable, once again a sharp decline in the number of resident stags has been recorded.

(Estimation of numbers: Red deer 300, ie. 260 hind herd, 40 stag herd (10 mature).

Area 4, Hawkcombe Valley, Porlock Common, Porlock Parks and Worthy Wood

This superb area of beautiful woodland and fine stretches of moorland has long been a stronghold for Red deer as well as a small population of Roe deer today. The woodlands offer ideal browsing and shelter for the deer, the majority of it being characteristic stunted oak, ancient and typical of Exmoor. In recent years a considerable amount of fencing has affected traditional runs of the Red deer in this area. With the fencing in of Shillett Wood and Berry Castle with no provision of deer leaps, the clear sweep that the deer used to enjoy from their woodlands to the open moor has been somewhat restricting for them especially hinds with young calves.

This area is my home and the place I know most intimately concerning deer. It has always been a stag area favoured by them in winter and summer. Though numbers are still reasonable, I would estimate a reduction of probably around half of the stags that were to be found in this area ten years ago. The majority of the remaining resident stags rut in the Horner and Dunkery districts and their reduction is also noticeable during this time with less vigorous and competitive ruts today.

(Estimation of numbers: Red deer 70, ie. 55 hind herd, 15 stag herd (7 mature).

Area 5, Coastal Area, Worthy Toll Road to Foreland Point

This area is a breathtaking stretch of the Exmoor coastline and generally known as the Culbone Cliffs. The hanging deciduous woodlands cling to these cliffs and grow down to the rocky seashore far below. It is a dangerous area to walk off the beaten track, being susceptible to regular land slides. For centuries, there must have been resident cliff Red deer that along with a few Roe deer are found in this area today. Some of these deer, especially the hinds, probably never leave these coastal haunts. The cliff stags that were once plentiful, took full advantage of the peaceful habitat the country afforded to them and over the years, I have seen some exceptional stags from this area. During the rut, the more adventurous of these stags would travel from their remote home to rut out on Exmoor.

Sadly in recent years the cliff Red deer have suffered a grave decline and today are but a fraction of their former glory. Large

A fine Culbone cliff (Area 5) stag rutting out on the moor.

stags, especially of the quality that was once seen, are all but gone. (Estimation of numbers: Red deer 100, ie. 85 hind herd, 15 stag herd (2 mature).

Area 6, all west of Lynmouth, north of the A39 to Blackmoor Gate to the National Park boundary

A superb area of Exmoor which offers ideal woodland habitat around the aptly named Woody Bay and in the Heddon Valley area. It is somewhat encouraging to report a slight recovery of late for the Red deer and with the appearance of a few Roe deer, it is a rewarding area for the devoted deer watcher.

(Estimation of numbers: Red deer 70, ie. 55 hind herd, 15 stag herd (5 mature).

Area 7, Forest of Exmoor or Parish of Simonsbath, area between Simonsbath to Lynmouth to Hawkcombe Head

This barren moorland area is the centre of Exmoor and a fine stronghold for deer. The habitat is grass (molinia) and heather moor as well as the grassland where the moor has been ploughed. Due probably to disturbance by people there has been a recent shift by the forest deer to the Brendon Valley and Lynmouth covers. The Forest of Exmoor was most famous for its spectacular herd of stags but during my time they have gradually declined in numbers and quality with survivors moving to pastures new.

(Estimation of numbers: Red deer 85, ie. 65 hind herd, 20 stag herd (5 mature).

Area 8, all west of Lynmouth B3223 to Simonsbath, to National Park boundary in the west.

This is another beautiful expanse of high heather and grass moorland fringed with farmland and a small amount of woodland cover in Hoar Oak and Farley Combe. This more remote and inaccessible part of Exmoor is only enjoyed to the full by the more determined walker or rider. This area was also once part of the ancient Forest of Exmoor.

The central feature of this part of the country is a high desolate grassy plateau called "The Chains". It is all above 1500 feet with the most prominent feature, Chains Barrow at 1599 feet. From this high vantage point one can enjoy wonderful views of the shape of Exmoor. The Chains is one great watershed, its surface a peat bog with any drainage prevented by a thin iron pan just below the surface. Average rainfall on the chains is the highest on Exmoor. Down on the coast it averages thirty five inches a year, while on the Chains it reaches the upper seventies. The Chains is the birthplace for Exmoor's two notable Rivers the Exe and the Barle.

With a lack of woodland shelter and its bleakness the area does not offer the best favoured type of habitat for deer. It has always been home for some residents but has never really been highly populated with them. Today Red deer can be found in certain parts, and some Roe deer.

In recent years there has been a marked increase in the number of Red deer harbouring in this district with the deer being seen in places where they have hardly been seen before. This is almost certainly the result of pressure and disturbance in other areas causing the deer to search for a more remote and undisturbed habitat.

(Estimation of numbers: Red deer 44, ie. 30 hind herd, 14 stag herd (4 mature).

Area 9, east of B396, to Wheddon Cross, north of the Brendon Hill Ridge Road to Dunster, Croydon Hill, Treborough and Monksilver

This large area takes in the northern half of the Brendon Hills. The habitat for deer in this area is woodland and farmland. The forestry on Croydon Hill is the largest area of commercial woodland on Exmoor. The area is notably the home for Exmoor's wild Fallow deer as well as Red and Roe deer. The Fallow deer came to live in the wild after the disbandment of Dunster Deer Park and Nettlecombe Court, around the Second World War and thrived due to the new covers that were planted at that time. Like the Fallow deer, Roe deer were also well suited to thriving in this sort of habitat and both species are found in this area today.

The Red deer in this area tend to favour the deciduous woodland notably in the area of the Cutcombe covers around Wheddon Cross. Before the Second World War, Red deer were plentiful throughout this area but to the present day, they have suffered a massive reduction in numbers.

(Estimation of numbers: 120 Red deer ie. 100 hind herd, 20 stag herd (4 mature).

Area 10, Quarme and Exe Valley on either side of the A396

The Exe Valley from Wheddon Cross down to the National Park boundary at the Pixton Estate below Dulverton, provides an abundance of mixed woodland habitat on both sides of the valley and is interwoven with farmland. Good numbers of Red deer and some Roe deer harbour in this valley. Within this area is the "League Against Cruel Sports'" most notable sanctuary at Baronsdown and Barlynch Wood. Like all of this organisation's land, it is not deer fenced and so the wild Red deer are free to come and go and the sanctuary is an important part of the deer of the district's range.

All of this valley area is a stronghold of major importance to the wild Red deer of Exmoor. The woodlands are their home and they also rely heavily on the goodwill of the Hunt - supporting landowners and farmers for their continued survival.

(Estimation of numbers: Red deer 400, ie. 350 hind herd, 50 stag herd (20 mature).

A fine stag following a hind out of Smallacombe and onto Culbone Hill (1979). There are no wild Red deer in this area today between Area 5 and 7.

A fine herd of forest stags (Area 7).

Area 11, south of Wheddon Cross to Exford, Great Staddon and Exe Valley

A smaller but reasonable deer area, for the most part it is farmland with some remaining heathland mainly on the steep valley sides where there is an abundance of bracken cover for the deer; the area only provides a small amount of woodland habitat. As well as the resident Red deer, Roe deer, though still a rarity, have been recently recorded.

(Estimation of numbers: Red deer 70, ie. 50 hind herd, 20 stag herd (5 mature).

Area 12, south of the Brendon Hill Ridge Road to National Park boundary, Brompton Regis, Haddon

Typical of Exmoor, this area is one of variety with farmland and woodland and a large remaining area of moorland on Haddon Hills. With the cover afforded on the southern slopes of the Brendon Hill and in the Haddon district it is ideal for the deer and has for centuries been a stronghold. Today there is also a well established Roe deer population.

The Haddon deer suffered a considerable amount of disturbance and loss of habitat within their home with the construction of Wimbleball Dam and the flooding of the valley above Hartford, but today there are still considerable numbers living in and around the district.

(Estimation of numbers: Red deer 100, ie. 80 hind herd, 20 stag herd (6 mature).

Area 13, The Barle Valley, Withypool to Dulverton and the Danesbrook

This area is the main centre and stronghold for southern Exmoor's deer with the abundance of woodland habitat afforded in the Barle valley. The country is an area of contrast and outstanding natural beauty with the woodlands, large sweeps of heathland in the Danesbrook area and on Winsford Hill, interwoven with farmland. Red and Roe deer are found living in this area, the Red deer predominating over a small population of Roe. Traditionally, it is a strong rutting area for the Red deer with a great deal of inter action between this area and the Red deer strongholds immediately south of the National Park boundary. This interaction is at a peak at the

27

time of the rut when more stags move into the area.
(Estimation of numbers: Red deer 180, ie. 150 hind herd, 30 stag herd (10 mature).

Area 14, Barle Valley, Simonsbath to Withypool

There has been a marked recent increase in Red deer numbers using this area. It has been much favoured by stags attracted to the peace and undisturbance of the area, a result of increased people pressure in old haunts such as in area 7.
(Estimation of numbers: Red deer 30, ie. 10 hind herd, 20 stag herd (10 mature).

Area 15, Withypool Hill to Molland Common to Twitchen

Across this area of moorland and farmland Red deer commute a great deal from south of the National Park and into Exmoor. The area is exposed with little woodland cover so fewer deer are resident but large numbers are regularly seen
(Estimation of numbers: Red deer 70, ie. 60 hind herd, 10 stag herd (3 mature).

Area 16, south of Fyldon Ridge to Heasely Mill

A good area for deer including fine woodland cover. Numbers fluctuate with the seasons and many of the deer that use this area have been included in adjoining areas.
(Estimation of numbers: Red deer 40, ie. 30 hind herd, 10 stag herd (4 mature).

Area 17, all south of Challacombe/Simonsbath Road to Bray

Typical of Exmoor, this area is a mixture of moorland, farmland and woodland in the top of the Bray valley. Once again there is considerable movement of deer and interaction over the National Park boundary. Due to woodland disturbance deer, especially stags, have been attracted to the moorland habitat in recent years.
(Estimation of numbers: Red deer 35, ie. 20 hind herd, 15 stag herd (5 mature).

DEER NUMBERS AND DISTRIBUTION

The composition and quality of the
wild Red deer herds on Exmoor

The result of the study of the numbers and distribution of the wild Red deer of Exmoor, was an estimated total of 1,834 head, resident within the Exmoor National Park. Unevenly distributed, with almost half of the population found harbouring in just three of the seventeen study areas, i.e. areas 3, 10 and 13. In these areas where deer were more plentiful, is found an abundance of deciduous woodland which the deer obviously depend on for food, shelter, preservation and sympathetic management of woodland with the deer's welfare in mind, is vitally important for their survival on Exmoor. Wholesale turning over of otherwise quiet, undisturbed woodlands to pheasant shooting on a large scale, poses a severe threat to the peaceful habitat of the deer.

Stag herd numbers were estimated to be 319, of which approximately 113 were observed to be of mature age and carrying a full grown head of antlers. To make an assessment of the complete breakdown of the sexes for Exmoor's wild Red deer, it is necessary to make an approximate estimation of the number of male deer living in the hind herds which obviously includes male calves, yearlings (knobbers), two year olds (prickets) and any adolescent young stags (spring stags) which have yet to leave the hind herd. For this I have made the following calculation:-

Hind Herds (Total 1,515)	Male	Female
50% mature hinds (of breeding age)		757.5
5% prickets and spring stags	75.75	
20% male calves, yearlings (knobbers)	303	
25% female calves, yearlings and adolescent females		378.75
Totals	378.75	1136.25

It is estimated that 378.75 of the hind herds are male deer and so adding on the stag herd numbers gives us the following result as regards to the balance of the sexes for the wild Red deer of Exmoor, Male = 697.75, Female = 1136.25.

The result of my survey indicates an imbalance of the sexes within the herds of wild Red deer on Exmoor. There is a shortage of males especially of large mature autumn stags. The decline of stags numbers has been a rapid and recent one, for ten years ago, when I began this intensive study, the situation was a much more healthy one.

Its effect on the herd is a general reduction in size and quality of large powerful stags. A high number of breeding hinds are mated with lesser and younger, untested stags which results in a poorer quality offspring and weakens the overall quality.

HINDS AND CALVING

Like all living creatures the reproduction of the species is the fundamental drive in Red deer. After mating during the autumn rut, the adult hind begins an eight month gestation period or on average 230 days. There is no delayed implantation of the egg to the ovary as occurs in the species of Roe deer.

The calf's development during gestation and the production of milk to rear it is a great drain on the hind's resources and in more impoverished conditions such as are found in the Highlands of Scotland, hinds give birth every other year. Although if conditions were more favourable, the hind is capable of producing a calf every year. From my study of individuals on Exmoor, who benefit from woodland habitat and better feeding, most adult hinds of three years old and over, do produce a calf every year.

Mid-June is the peak calving time for the Red deer. The majority of hinds that are ready to give birth, wander away from their resident herd to choose a suitable calving spot. Experienced hinds have their regular area and their giving birth can take place in the same cover and small area every year. The hind makes full use of cover available within her range when choosing a calving spot and it also must be secluded and offer a good chance of escape for a young calf if discovered by predators and so wire fences and

New born calf in the heather.

impregnable cover is avoided.

On the high moor a favourite calving spot is amongst the rushes at the head of a moorland stream and where more cover is available bracken beds are the first choice, though the hind will use heather and gorse and whortleberry cover. In open woodland the hind may simply choose a hollow or depression on the woodland floor. Every year, there are a few hinds who give birth well before the end of May and indeed some very late births. I once found a newborn calf on the 8th August. The birth can take place at any time of the day or night and it is almost unknown for a hind to be found in difficulty while calving. The only incident of this kind I have known was on Tivington Hill (Area 2) when a Veterinary was called to the aid of a hind that was found in difficulty.

The birth of single calves are the rule for the Red deer and the occurrence of twins is a great rarity. Immediately following the birth, the hind licks and cleans the calf and by scent forms a strong bond between herself and her offspring. Preceding this, she will consume the placenta or birth sac. Within the first hour the calf endeavours to struggle up onto its legs and take its first unsteady steps. Instinctively and encouraged by mother, the calf is soon suckling and taking its first feed.

Calf suckling while mother takes an interest in another hind's calf.

When all is well, the hind leaves her calf lying in its place of concealment and she goes away to feed and drink and recover from the birth. Contact between her herd and other mothers is soon renewed though they are loath to stray too far from their calves and remain extremely anxious and nervous for their young. Many newborn calves are left hidden throughout all the daylight hours, mothers returning to them at dusk to be with them during the night, then once again leaving them at dawn. The occurrence of daytime visits to the calf, only takes place in more remote areas where there is less human disturbance and chance of the hind giving away the secret of her calf's location.

The newborn calves have large light spots on their dark brown coats and when lying hidden, depend on their lack of scent and camouflage to protect them from dangers in what is the most vulnerable time of their lives, the first few days. The numbers lost to foxes, stray dogs and over-heating due to dehydration is in my opinion, quite considerable on Exmoor. The camouflage of the new-born is often described as sunlight on fallen leaves as they do give a somewhat vivid dappled effect as the light shines on them. *See illustration.* For the first few days, the new born calves lie with their heads to the ground. It cannot be over-emphasised, that should one

Sunlight on fallen leaves.

33

discover a new born calf, it should never be touched as this can lead to rejection by mother and in the interest of the deer, time spent with the calf should be kept at a minimum. The assumption that a calf has been abandoned simply because it is lying on its own, is obviously misguided. A molested calf can emit a loud high pitched bleat which the hind immediately responds to by coming to its aid. Hinds will tackle predators like foxes to protect their young.

The hind's milk is extremely nutritious and the calf rapidly increases in weight and strength. After three to four days, it adopts a stronger, head-up position and is able to follow mother for short distances. The calf will also choose its own place to lie and is capable of jumping up and away in the wake of danger. When the calf is strong enough, usually in the second week, it follows mother to the main hind herd. The young calves that meet in the herd play like lambs indulging in various games of chase and racing when the deer are at peace. The hinds are extra alert for danger at this time and their abrupt loud barking call is heard more frequently than at any other time of the year. On occasions, some hinds will leave their calf with an old hind, who takes the role of a nanny, as mother goes away to feed. In the summer of 1979, on Culbone Hill (Area 5) I observed one old hind in the woodland who was surrounded by no less than six spotted calves that were left in her care.

From the moment the calf is born, life is a rapid learning process, assisted by instincts. As the calf grows up, he learns the way of the deer and their home and how to survive. The calf soon learns to mimic mother's feeding habits and within a few weeks is supplementing mother's milk by browsing on herbage. It is five to six months before the calf is completely weaned from mother. A few unlucky calves lose their mothers in early life. At four months a wild Red deer calf has some chance of survival on Exmoor without mother, depending on the severity of its first winter.

Also at four months the young calf is losing its woolly baby coat and with it the spots gradually fade away as the calf takes on a normal deer appearance.

THE DEER'S FOOD

Deer are ruminants, browsing for a time, then lying up to chew the cud. Their diet is varied and includes almost everything green, from the plants and herbs of the woodland and moor, to gardens and farmland, where they are accessible. The deer's food greatly affects their quality and it is a natural instinct for the deer to make the best of the food availability within their range. Red deer are capable of jumping considerable heights and squeezing through seemingly impossible gaps to gain access to food.

The history of the Red deer in Britain highlights how this gregarious wild animal has been slowly rendered extinct, as an unwelcome agricultural pest, coupled with the loss of habitat. In the Highlands of Scotland, the wild Red deer's main stronghold, vast tracts of deer country have been separated from forestry and farmland by long, continuous, high deer-proof fencing, eradicating much of the deer and agriculture conflict.

In comparison to Scotland, the wild Red deer's West Country stronghold is tiny. Exmoor still retains some of its high moorland wilderness but the majority of the Red deer's habitat is interwoven with farmland. 16,000 acres is woodland and 40,000 acres is remaining heather and grass moorland on which the deer also compete with a rising number of grazing sheep and cattle, and ponies in their natural habitat. Unlike the Highland deer forests, which are usually under the control of one authority and devoted almost entirely to the deer, Exmoor is owned by thousands of different people, many of them being small acreage farmers. The area is also criss-crossed with numerous roads, connecting many villages. Feeding on agricultural land has been a constant threat to the species' survival in the West Country. Save for the reinstatement of stag hunting, over a hundred years ago on Exmoor, the species would almost certainly, not have survived as they have done to the present day. The situation has not changed and the continued survival of Exmoor's wild Red deer over the whole of their present natural range, still depends heavily on the tolerance of hunt-supporting farmers to deer, when they look to feed on their land.

Exmoor's deer enjoy easier conditions than their Scottish Highland relatives who endure harsh winters and are more exposed. On most Highland deer forests the herds are given supplementary food. With milder winters and the shelter of woodlands as well as choice feeding, the Exmoor deer are not artificially fed, yet they are

generally of better condition.

Despite this, the abundance of new spring growth is welcomed by the deer on Exmoor, after the long winter. In the woodlands, they browse on the fresh plant, herb and shrub growth and the patches of tender new grass. The common blackberry or bramble shoots are a woodland favourite and on the moor, the fresh heather and whortleberry shoots. On farmland, young grass fields are a magnet for the deer in the spring. These fields are even more to their liking as they are not stocked with the farm animals and so the deer get the first pickings.

A fine stag browsing from a mountain ash.

Although the wild Red deer will feed at any time, it is at night when they are most active in farmers' fields and dawn and dusk is the most likely time to observe the deer on the move. Stags are bolder than the hinds when breaking into fields as the hinds have the handicap of young at foot, who cannot manage to jump the wire fences. The woodlands frequented by the wild Red deer have all the signs of their presence, not only from their slot marks (hoof marks), lying beds and droppings, but also the evidence of where they have been browsing. The deer have eight biting teeth in the lower jaw but only a hard gum pad above. Vegetation is half-bitten through, then torn away. They also leave a distinct browsing line on hedges and trees at the limit of where they can manage to reach up.

A deciduous woodland which supports wild Red deer can easily provide for a reasonable number but when numbers are too high, the natural regeneration of the wood is impaired by the deer constantly browsing the young saplings when they are at feeding level. A healthy, tolerable number of deer in a wood do a lot of good by keeping the brambles and ground cover down, and encouraging re-generation and keep the deer tracks clear, making it a pleasant wood to walk in, a wood that otherwise would be choked.

As the summer progresses many of the grass fields are now stocked with ewes and lambs. The deer concentrate more on the fields that are left for mowing and also cereal crops. These often provide enough cover for the deer to lie up in them all day. Very often a few deer will take up residence for several weeks. When feeding in a cornfield, a hind will economically nip off the ears like a rabbit, while a stag will draw all the corn off the stalk in one go.

Unless they are properly fenced, all gardens and allotments near to the Red deer's home may be visited by the deer. Stags can dig up potatoes with their antlers and deer like most vegetables. Fruit trees are also to the deer's liking, especially apples. The cemetery at Porlock is regularly visited by deer at night not only for the fresh grass but they also take the flowers off the graves. It is noticed that yellow flowers, especially daffodils, are never touched.

After a summer of plenty, the Red deer are in good condition and stags especially, are carrying fat surpluses which they will use up during the frenzied activity of the autumn rut. Chestnuts attract many deer to the woodlands at this time of the year.

The leaner months of winter see a natural slowing down in the appetites of the deer. The food available on the moors and in the woods is of low energy value by the end of the winter and the deer are careful not to use up more energy in the search for food than they can find. During the day, they lie up for hours avoiding the energy-sapping, biting wind by choosing sheltered spots and taking full advantage of the sun when it shines. Fields of swedes and turnips are especially vulnerable to deer at this time of the year. This crop, which is grown for the sheep in the spring, is at risk for long periods.

A great deal of time and trouble is devoted by the farmer to deter deer and strengthen hedges and fences. A variety of objects are hung around vulnerable fields to deter the deer such as bags, tape and deer skins. These seldom deter the deer for long and I have even seen Red deer feeding unperturbed beside a crow scarer that was going off at regular intervals.

In winter the deer food supply in woodlands can become extremely short, but they never completely run out of something to eat. Last resorts are the bitter and what must be unpalatable, ivy and holly leaves. The deer will nibble at the lichen on the trees and dig in snow and the ground for food and roots. Deer will eat stinging nettles and I once witnessed a hind that was cleverly pulling up the old fern stalks twisting them round in her mouth and just eating the root nodules.

Lean times for an Exmoor stag.

THE RUT

The mating period of the Red deer is known as the rut and takes place during the autumn months. Around early September begins a gradual build-up until in mid-October the rut is at its peak. Firstly hind herds gather up and advertise their existence around traditional rutting stand areas. Wet areas in the districts the hinds frequent are turned into muddy wallows, which on Exmoor are known as soiling pits. These can vary in size from a small puddle on a path or deer track to the large traditional soiling pits at spring heads at the top of moorland combes. The deer's wallowing or soiling is a great relief and refreshment from the plague of ticks and lice which have tormented them throughout the heat of summer. The start of this intensive soiling activity is also triggered by the moulting of the deer's summer coat for a darker autumn appearance. Young juvenile males still living in the hind herds and yet to leave their female cousins can be observed at this time of the year displaying premature rutting behaviour such as chasing hinds and attempting to "balve" the mating call of the wild Red deer.

Within the stag herds during September the mood is becoming one of increased discontentment with each other's company, caused by a

Early October and a fine Exmoor stag, known as Royal, has returned to his favoured rutting area.

gradual rising of the testosterone level, the male sexual hormone which causes an increase in sparring matches and frustrated displays of violence. By the third week in September stag herds have all but parted from each other's company and left their summer haunts to travel in search of hinds, or in the case of mature established stags, to return to defend their dominance in an area and begin the year's rutting campaign.

Impetuous young spring stags are first to join the hind herds at the end of September. Older more experienced stags stall their arrival until the beginning of October, saving their energy and strength until the first of the hinds are coming into season. These big mature stags soon oust the young pretenders and juvenile males in the herds with their arrival on the scene. For the young stags it is not the end of the rut for they will travel the country in search of unattached hinds or remain on the fringe of a master stag's rutting stand, persistently attempting to steal in on his hinds and try to run one away.

Around mid-October when the rut is at a peak, master stags emit their challenging rutting call loudly and most regularly. On Exmoor the call of the rutting stag is known as balving as opposed to roaring or belling as it is also referred to in other parts of the British Isles. The sound all the same is a deep uninterrupted note lasting several seconds and varying in pitch and often followed immediately by a number of short grunts. It is an eerie sound, especially when heard on a still night, when the sound can carry and be heard a mile or more away.

A stag's balve is his statement of his dominance and his challenge to rivals. In one way balving is a safety valve with many rutting disputes settled by just a balving match avoiding violent confrontations. It is a wonderful experience to hear the balving of stags in the wild, especially when a number of individuals are regularly calling and answering each other in the same area. At this time of the year on Exmoor the moorland roads and pull-in spots at likely places are busy in the evening with people out especially to hear the stags. As well as a challenge, the balving of a stag is greatly intensified by the presence of a hind at the height of her season. The balving probably also serves to stimulate a hind to mate.

The shedding of the velvet around the end of July will also induce the occasional stag to emit a half-hearted premature balve, I have only heard two such balves on Exmoor and the reason for this occurrence is one of the mysteries in the deer world. Balving matches fail to settle all rutting disputes and serious fights can ensue

A stag's balve is his statement of his dominance and his challenge to rivals.

when two equally matched stags decide to take their vocal disagreement one step further. This involves the two stags moving in and inspecting each other at close quarters. The ritual for these stags is to do a parallel walk, keeping a set distance apart and walking forward and back eyeing each other up and down. Suddenly one stag goes for the other and a head to head battle begins. It is the ultimate test of strength and agility. Hinds nonchalantly look on as the clashes of antlers resound across the moor. Serious wounds to the head and neck are a common result of fighting, including a danger of eyes being gored. Points of antlers are often broken off and occasionally a whole antler is left hanging just by the skin as the pedicle breaks on the skull. Most fights are over in a few minutes. Fights to the death are a great rarity, a weakening, defeated stag is usually able to turn tail and beat a hasty retreat. The most dangerous stag in a fight is the one-antlered individual for instead of locking with the rival the one antler pierces through the guard like a lance.

A harem of 40 or more deer is quite exceptional for a stag to acquire and successfully defend throughout the peak of the rut. Obviously not all of these are mature hinds of breeding age. Due to the amount of human disturbance today on Exmoor it is even harder for a stag to hold such a number. Peak rutting activity takes place during the hours of darkness. Only in more remote and inaccessible parts of the deer's home can the deer continue with their rutting rituals during the day without feeling threatened by giving away their presence. During all of the rut, stags find little time for feeding and rest. Hinds are chased and pursued relentlessly and eventually the stag is rewarded when the courted hind eventually stands for him. The covering is over in a few seconds; to witness such a sight is a rarity in the wild as this is more often a night time affair. The only times I have witnessed a stag serving a hind on Exmoor was either at dawn or dusk.

The autumn rut is the event in the Red deer calendar and the most rewarding time for the deer watcher. Stags are at large, preoccupied and rather more off-guard than usual. Their best defence is their harem of ever-alert hinds that are quick to warn the rutting stag of danger. Soiling pits are now also the focus of attention for stags, mainly to mark as their own with scent from urine and glands. They also indulge in soiling for their general refreshment and to give themselves a formidable dark muddy appearance.

The autumn weather is often far from ideal for observing the rut, gales and rain are commonplace, often accompanied by thick fog driving the most ardent of deer watchers from the moor. In such

Royal with a large harem.

weather deer also seek the shelter of valleys and woodlands where they will forage for chestnuts, an autumn favourite. On still days autumn sunshine will guarantee the Red deer will be out basking on the moor.

With their fear and respect for man, wild Red deer are not dangerous to approach and be near to at any time during the rut. In my experience I have never been threatened by a stag on Exmoor and it is unknown for anyone to have been harmed by the deer in peaceful conditions. In the hunting field, there are a few records of huntsmen having been gored and injured by the cornered stags especially when they are standing at bay. In the case of captive deer the situation is quite different, especially when stags are restricted to small enclosures during the run up to the rut. The stag in this situation can become extremely dangerous, due to his frustration at not being able to travel and roam in search of mates. The stag will then attack anything that moves at any time and there have been many fatalities involving the keepers of the deer. On Exmoor the most unnerving experience I had with the deer took place during the rut of 1987. I had stalked and got extremely close to a large stag and eight hinds. It was early morning and the stag was at a peak of rutting frenzy, balving loudly, pawing the ground with his feet and

Soon to return to their old haunts.

43

antlers and chasing his hinds. Suddenly, one hind that was being pursued, headed straight towards where I was concealed and passed me within touching distance, I ducked down as I heard the stag coming. He suddenly froze as he caught my scent, leapt into the air and jumped clean over me to race away and leave me quite flabbergasted.

One stag that was seen to have lost out in a fight on Dunkery in 1979, took his vengeance out on a sheep standing by and gored it to death. Another rare occurrence is for a rutting stag to have his patience so tried by the hind he is pursuing, that he will occasionally give up and gore her to death. Two fighting stags have been known to get their antlers inseparably locked together while fighting and for the two to perish from slow starvation.

For the most part, the rut is over by mid-November, stags gradually retiring from the scene and reforming their original stag herds back in their old haunts. The seed is sown for another year. For a few stags their rut can linger on to Christmas and beyond, their interest fuelled by a few hinds that had failed to be covered during their oestrus and returning again into a late season. This is a situation that is more prevalent on Exmoor due to the present state of the herd, a shortage of large mature tested stags to go around.

ANTLERS

Few people realise that unlike the horns of sheep and cattle that are permanent, the antlers of deer are shed annually and re-grown in approximately four months every year. The re-growth of deer antlers is the fastest grown structure in any animal and in the case of a large mature stag he is growing between ten to fourteen pounds of antler in a third of a year.

Antler shedding involves a great deal of wastage and in areas of calcium deficiency such as in the Highlands of Scotland, the cast antlers are consumed by the deer, but in the less deprived conditions on Exmoor, I have little evidence of this occurrence. The antler cycles of the various species of deer in the world that we can observe today are the result of millions of years of evolutionary change and the antler cycles are closely interconnected with the night and daylight hours wherever the deer may live. Why the deer shed their antlers at all is probably best explained by an evolutionary theory that the antlers of earliest deer were thought not to be hard bone but made of a cartilage-like substance and vulnerable to frostbite during the climatic changes of the world. The deer slowly evolved to replacing damaged and lost antler from the severe weather with a harder more

A mature stag with a fine head attire has proved himself to be fit and a survivor.

45

Mature old stag in an Exmoor woodland with a large, heavy pair of antlers.

resistant substance hard antler, until eventually they were shedding and re-growing a whole pair of antlers in one season.

For the Red deer only the male, the stag, has antlers. In some species ie, Reindeer, both the male and female develop them whilst in some other species neither sex has antlers at all. The Red deer like most temperate species shed their antlers in the spring and re-grow them during the summer months. One exception is in the case of Britain's other native species the Roe deer, where the Roe buck sheds his antlers in late autumn and re-grows them throughout the winter months.

Conditions and food availability govern the rate at which deers antlers develop in their lives and their eventual size and quality and the age at which full antler development is achieved. Breeding and heredity also play a major role.

The main role of stags' antlers is for a display during the mating time such as the elaborate colourful plumage of a male bird of paradise. A mature stag with a fine head attire has proved himself to be fit and a survivor, he has made the best of food availability and is of good breeding. Nature ensures that the next generation of Red deer is of the best possible quality. As well as the antlers' sexual role, they also play a vital role in individual recognition, as fighting weapons, as tools for digging and scratching.

A few stags fail to grow any antlers in their lives. On Exmoor these are described as Knott Stags or in Scotland as Hummels. The reason for this can be due to hormonal or genetic abnormality or damage to the testes. Without the burden and stress associated with antler growth every year, knott stags can achieve a much heavier body weight and condition. Even without antlers, knott stags are also surprisingly successful during the rut with their impressive body weight and ability to fight by rearing up and swiping with their front legs. From the results of experiment, the offspring of knott stags are no more likely to be antlerless in later life than the progeny of a normal antlered stag.

Shedding or Mewing

Between the top of the pedicle on the stag's skull and just below the crown of the stag's antlers is a live dead interface known as the oestoclast layer. Early in the year the oestoclast activity begins with cells beginning to break down. By the spring the antlers are only held on by a small amount of unbroken bone on this layer and soon, depending on the age of the stag the antlers fall cleanly away. The older the stag the earlier he will shed his antlers (see Table 1-2 Antler Development). The earliest shedding date I recorded on Exmoor was on the 11th March. Most stags shed their two antlers some distance apart whilst a few shed their pair of antlers simultaneously, see Chapter entitled "Stag Horning".

ANTLER RENEWAL

The re-growth of antlers begins immediately after the old antlers have been shed. Just after shedding the top of the pedicles appear red and raw. After a day or two the layer then turns bluey and healed. Then immediately the new velvet growth begins and after a week of shedding approximately half an inch of re-growth is visible on the stag's head.

The regrowth is a mass of sensitive cartilage tissue, richly permeated with blood and covered by a protective skin called velvet. The main blood vessels that feed the growth tips of the antlers are just under the outer velvet covering. The velvet is covered with short hairs a few millimetres long which does give it a texture similar to mole skin. In the case of the Roe buck who grows his antlers throughout the winter months, the velvet has much longer hairs upon it for protection from frostbite.

During the antler renewal, growth only takes place on top of the main stem and on the top of the branches or points as each one is developed up this main stem. Re-grown antler is at its final width or size of beam once complete. To re-grow a pair of antlers in what is a remarkably short space of time, four months of summer, requires

Mature stag showing antler renewal in the second week after shedding his antlers.

A fine bunch of stags in late May in various stages of antler renewal.

large mineral (calcium) resources on the part of the animal. These cannot possibly come from just the deer's food and so the deer also draw immensely on their skeletal reserves.

As mentioned, deer in deprived conditions are forced to consume cast antlers and sometimes bones to combat calcium deficiency. On Exmoor this is not found, for shed antlers can be found in the deer's home only slightly chewed by almost certainly small rodents and having remained there for years. The same antlers in a calcium deficient area such as in the Highlands of Scotland would quickly be chewed to a stub by the deer.

While antlers are growing and in velvet the heat from blood close to the surface of the antlers is extremely attractive to flies and at times can cause the stag extreme agitation. Occasionally stags are forced to go to a river for the relief of plunging themselves in. It has been thought that apart from the disadvantage of the growing antlers attracting flies they do act as a cooling system for the deer during the heat of the summer, acting something like a radiator expelling heat.

There is a considerable amount of variation in the colour of the velvet between individual stags ranging from almost black to a very light grey. It is common although not a set rule that the older the stag the lighter grey his antlers in velvet will appear. Growing

49

Mature stag in velvet hiding up in a bracken bed.

antlers are often damaged by knocks and bangs and can be completely severed. As a living part of the stag this must be extremely painful. To minimise the chance of damage to growing antlers the stag prefers, if possible, to lie in open cover such as in fern beds. When having to move at speed through dense cover a stag with a large head can skilfully lay his antlers back onto his back. At this point it seems appropriate to highlight the cruel practice in some countries of cutting velvet from growing deer's antlers as the velvet is highly valued as an aphrodisiac.

The time for a stag to fray his antlers depends on his age and the conditions he is living in (see Tables 1 and 2). The blood supply dries up and the velvet dries and withers as the antlers solidify. It is a time of intense irritation for the stag. On a few occasions I have seen stags with their faces covered in blood as they begin to fray or strip off the velvet. The spot where a stag chooses to brash and clean the velvet from his antlers is aptly on Exmoor known as the fraying stock. He may use anything for this purpose. The most common is a gorse bush or withy, a young fir sapling or a low branch of any tree. The damage the stags cause to trees on Exmoor at this time is minimal and of little significance as stag numbers are low and widely distributed.

With careful inspection it is possible though extremely difficult to find shed velvet where a stag has frayed. Stags have been seen on occasions eating this velvet and even eating the velvet off another stag's antlers. When first out of velvet the stag's antlers appear a light copper colour. Soon with regular rubbing the antlers become darker in appearance. The stags also indulge in frequent antler rubbing to familiarise themselves with their new head attire.

The colour and texture of the stag's antlers is a good indicator to the type of habitat that the stag is resident to. When living close to peat bogs such as are found on the high moor, the antlers can become extremely dark, almost black, whilst a woodland stag's antlers are a rich dark brown with highly polished white tips.

With maturity the stag's antlers acquire more pearling upon them (a rough texture) which is easier to darken when fraying — a reason why many of the lesser spring stag's antlers remain smooth and white.

An Exmoor stag with a perfect head, brow, bay, trey and three points on top. A twelve pointer known as Royal.

TABLE 1 – ANTLER DEVELOPMENT OF AN EXMOOR STAG

Habitat, moorland heath (some woodland & farmland) poorest of feeding

AGE (YRS)	0	1	2	3	4	5	6	7	8	9	10	11	12	13	14	15	16
JUNE	CALF IS BORN					SHEDS										FRAYS	FRAYS
JULY					SHEDS									FRAYS	FRAYS		
AUGUST													FRAYS				
SEPT									FRAYS		FRAYS	FRAYS					
OCT							FRAYS			FRAYS							
NOV		FRAYS	FRAYS	FRAYS		FRAYS		FRAYS									
DEC	PEDICLES START TO GROW (SEE FIG 1)	BUTTON SIZED FIRST ANTLERS	(button)	PRICKET (BROW) UPRIGHT	(BROW)(B-T4) UPRIGHT (B+4)	(B-T)(B-T.1)(B-T2) UPRIGHT (B+4)	(B-T2)(B-T2)	(B-T2)(B-T2)	(RIGHTS.2 a top)(B-T2)	(RIGHTS a top)	(RIGHTS)(RIGHTS)	(RIGHTS.2)(B-T2)	(B-T2)(B-T2)	(B-T2)(B-T.1)	(B-T) UPRIGHT (B+4)(BT.4)	(B+4)(BT.4) UPRIGHT	(BROW) UPRIGHT
JAN		STARTS FIRST ANTLER GROWTH	SECOND ANTLER GROWTH														
FEB			SHEDS BUTTON ANTLERS						SHEDS	SHEDS							
MARCH				PRICKET ANTLERS ARE SHED				SHEDS			SHEDS	SHEDS				SHEDS	SHEDS
APRIL						SHEDS	SHEDS						SHEDS	SHEDS	SHEDS		
MAY			FRAYS			SHEDS	SHEDS										

(SPRING STAG) (AUTUMN STAG) GOING BACK →

52

TABLE 2 – ANTLER DEVELOPMENT OF AN EXMOOR STAG

Habitat, woodland, farmland, some moorland, average to good feeding

B = Brow point, B = Bay point, T = Trey point

AGE (YRS)	0	1	2	3	4	5	6	7	8	9	10	11	12	13	14	15	16
JUNE	CALF IS BORN																
JULY		STARTS FIRST ANTLER GROWTH															FRAYS
AUG							FRAYS										
SEPT						FRAYS											
OCT					FRAYS												
NOV		FRAYS		FRAYS													
DEC		PRICKET												(SPRING STAG)			
JAN			PRICKET ANTLERS ARE SHED														
FEB			SHEDS						SHEDS								
MARCH							SHEDS			SHEDS	SHEDS	SHEDS	SHEDS	SHEDS	SHEDS	SHEDS	SHEDS
APRIL						SHEDS											
MAY				SHEDS	SHEDS												

PEDICLES START TO GROW — SEE FIG(1)

(SPRING STAG)   (AUTUMN STAG) ——→←—— (GOING BACK) ——→

ANTLER DEVELOPMENT

The way in which a male Red deer develops his head of antlers throughout his life is a fascinating study. There is a tremendous variation from one individual to another depending a great deal on the conditions and food availability. Each stag's antler growth is an individual blue print never ever the same as another set of antlers or ever seen exactly the same before or to be repeated again. Despite shedding and regrowing these antlers annually, recognisable characteristics are often retained enabling the deer watcher to recognise individuals year after year - invaluable in the study of wild deer.

Tables 1 and 2 show examples of antler development on Exmoor under different conditions. Table 1 shows a stag's antler development living in deprived conditions whilst Table 2 is of a stag living under more improved conditions. To understand how critical conditions and feeding are to antler development, it is best highlighted by the speed and remarkable antler growth that male Red deer achieve in the more cushioned conditions found in Deer Parks and Deer Farms. For their first head, many of the stags under these improved conditions can grow and achieve what would take a stag under the most favourable of Exmoor conditions at least four to

Heading for cover.

five years to achieve. It is not uncommon for the Deer Park stag to possess a 12 pointer head at three years old. That on Exmoor can take the stag nine years to achieve and for some, as in Table 1, three a-top was never attained. The all-time West Country record stag head for a wild deer was a twenty-two pointer, whilst in some parks this sort of head is not unusual.

Antler growth in male Red deer is influenced by the secretion of testosterone, the male sexual hormone and its secretion from the testes takes place during the deer's adolescence. Two bony columns grow from the skull of the deer which are called the pedicles. Under Exmoor conditions the pedicles, progress of pushing up through the skin on the deer's head is noticeable between eight and twelve months old. The first antler growth for the young male Exmoor Red deer commences at the start of the second year when the protruding top of the pedicle is covered in the protective skin velvet and antlers begin to grow. The amount of first antler growth depends on the conditions and it can be anything from two tiny button-sized growths to long spikes at least four inches long. Note the deer in Table 1 living under deprived conditions only attained the button-sized antler growth in his first growth during his second year and grew pricket antlers in his second antler growth during his third year.

As the stag matures he grows a longer main stem of antler each growing season with an increase every year until maturity of branches or points. The examples of Tables 1 and 2 are by no means a set rule as to antler growth on Exmoor, merely two typical fictitious examples. The term spring stag on Exmoor describes a young stag who is growing and developing his head at three to six years old. A mature stag on Exmoor is described as an autumn stag and should normally possess three points up each main stem of antler and usually the stem at the top has branched into two (see Table 1, Age 9 years, Table 2, Age 6 years). The amount of increase in size and points of the stag's head is again determined by conditions and feeding. Under deprived conditions, as in Example Table 1, the stag never achieved more than all the rights and two a-top whilst in Table 2 under improved conditions, the stag went on to achieve all the rights and five points on the top of each antler. Weakening with old age has its effect on the stag's ability to retain vigorous antler growth every year and the deterioration of the stag's antlers on Exmoor is described as "going back". This process will also be hastened by impoverished conditions as in the example Table 1 stag that began to go back at 11 years old. With better conditions Table 2 stag's going back process was much more prolonged with the stag able to grow a vigorous head up to 13 years old before the rigours of the wild took its toll.

This has been the merest sketch of the ways in which stags' antlers develop throughout their lives. There are no set rules and with such variations possible it is probably best to highlight the usual normal occurrences and the pitfalls to beware of in the study of stags' heads. The Brow Point, the first of the rights up the antler is usually the first point to develop from the main stem during a young stag's antler development. It is fairly rare for this not to be the case and in the mature stag's head it is the rarest point to be missing. The presence of a Brow Point that has forked into two is a sign of health and excellent living. In the case of an extremely old stag whose head is well gone back he is more likely to still have good Brow Points than any other point.

In contrast the Bay Point, the second of the rights on the stag's head is the point that is most likely to be absent. For the stag developing his head, it is most likely to be the last point for him to achieve before he reaches maturity. In many cases it is never grown and the head carried by the mature stag throughout his prime, is always Brow-Trey with whatever on top. In the process of going-back the Bay Point is the most common of points to be lost from the head during these years. The presence of vigorous Bay Point on a mature stag or good bay points on any growing stag is a sign of good quality and the animal that should always be preserved as the quality individual.

The Trey Point, the third up of the stag's rights is usually the second to develop on a spring stag's growing head. Once the stag's head is mature it is rare to see the Trey Point missing. In the process of going-back, the Trey Points are not normally lost until the later stages. I have known double trey points to occur but this is a great rarity. After the rights if all of them develop, the number of top points depend on the stag's conditions and quality which also governs the rate of development. Four points gained in one year was the most any of the Exmoor stags I have studied achieved. For an Exmoor stag today to achieve all his rights and five points on the top of each antler is quite exceptional.

Heads of antlers rarely develop symmetrically or are such in maturity ie. a stag's head is more likely to have a different number of points on the two antlers. Another interesting observation in this study is the swopping of uneven numbers of top points. For example the four and three a-top stag is quite likely to carry the four a-top on the right antler and three a-top on the left antler and reverse this situation the next year and continue to regularly swop the top points over.

After maturity the ageing process known as going back is just as varied and complex as the way in which the stags' heads develop. Going back either shows itself in the stunting and loss of either the rights or top points or both. The bay point being the most vulnerable of the rights to being lost at the start of the process. On the top of the antlers, like the withering of an ageing tree, the old stag ceases to have the strength and vitality to quite complete such a rapid required growth in such a short time and it is often the completion of vigorous well-formed top points that is left wanting. They become stunted and often grossly clumped together and form what is often described on Exmoor as cup tops. In extreme old age, which for an Exmoor stag would be fifteen years and over, the stag's head can eventually deteriorate and go back to merely brow and upright like the points he once possessed when he was once a young spring stag. This occurrence is more common in the deprived conditions of parts of the Highlands of Scotland where such stags are described as switches. Fifteen years old is exceptional for a stag in the vigours of the wild but in the cushioned environment of Deer Parks, stags if not culled, can easily live to a much greater age. One can be mistaken that a stag is going back due to old age when it can be the result of the deer having a poor summer that particular year. All the signs of going back may well be seen but as is the case of numerous examples I have observed, there is no reason why the situation, as it often does, will not improve the next year after a better summer of feeding.

Apart from the normal malformed heads that are the result of damage when the antlers are growing and in velvet, some deformities are clearly the result of genetic abnormality. For the Red deer one of the rarest and strangest of these is the antler that splits and grows into two. Usually this happens just above the brow point. The occurrence of this freak often gives rise to the three antlered stag rumour. In the few examples of this I have seen, normal points were always growing from the one stem and the double stem took the form of a long freak point usually growing from low down on the other main stem and from the back. The point can grow as long as the normal branched main stem. Other freak heads of note I have observed and studied nearly always involve points growing backwards. Of all the claims of a genuine three antlered stag observed, I have yet to see one that possesses three pedicles and crowns on one skull.

As seen from the varied patterns and forms of stags' antler development and the rate at which they grow, there are many pitfalls to assessing the age of a male Red deer solely from the study of his antlers. Conditions and climate have played the major role in their development as well as the variation in quality of breeding from one individual to another. A wild stag carrying a head with say eight points, a brow, trey two a-top, could be anything from five to sixteen years old.

Overall I have recorded a general decline in antler quality on Exmoor. The average stag's head is much smaller than it used to be. This is certainly the result of the general quality reduction of the herds but in some ways this decline is surprising. The result of moorland ploughing has meant the availability of improved feeding, especially for the high moorland deer and the general use of nitrate to improve grasslands has meant an improvement in feeding for all Exmoor deer. It seems apparent that these benefits have been heavily offset by increased competition for feeding on the remaining moorland areas, not only from the huge increase in other herbivores, the sheep, cattle and ponies, but also from the higher concentrations of deer numbers congregating in the diminishing availability of safe undisturbed areas of suitable habitat. This is highlighted by the much better quality deer that are found in fringe areas of Exmoor where conditions are so much better with much less competition for feeding.

DEER CONTROL ON EXMOOR

One could not imagine a more complex situation concerning the control over a wild Red deer population than the one that exists on Exmoor.

Complications begin immediately concerning land ownership. Though a "National Park" by name suggests a nation-owned preserve and the wildlife heavily protected; the land is actually under multi private land ownership. A wild deer on Exmoor receives no more lawful protection than a deer in any other part of England.

Preservation of deer is quite a voluntary obligation of any Exmoor landowner whose personal attitude to them is critical, given that there is not existent an overall commission to look after the deer's welfare and English laws over hunting and shooting are far more lax than other European countries. Much of Exmoor is cultivated and agricultural and there is little to stop an owner of such land exterminating the animal as just another unwanted pest. Given this situation, one might wonder how Exmoor's wild Red deer continue to survive. The habitat of the area is to the deer's liking with large tracts of heathland and heavily wooded valleys and some extremely inaccessible expanses, mainly on the coast and areas of large coniferous commercial forestry. Such habitat though has not staved their extinction from other such areas in England. One certainty for Exmoor's deer is that their survival over their remaining range has been and still remains heavily dependent on a level of preservation afforded to them for hunting. The Devon and Somerset Stag hounds' continued existence is the major incentive of private landowners to preserve the quarry of the sport they enjoy. This sport may be justifiably met with opposition on ethical grounds but when one unbiasedly considers the uniqueness of a large majority of farmers and landowners altogether, in one area of the English countryside, quite voluntarily ensuring the future of some Red deer to hunt, then one realises the importance of the continuation of hunting in the absence of laws to replace this level of preservation.

Some of Exmoor is owned by conservation bodies ie. National Trust, National Park etc.

No future policies would permit the extermination of all Red deer on lands belonging to these bodies no matter what but on the moor where the deer are wide ranging, the goodwill of the neighbouring farmers is vital. The National Trust on Exmoor own some of the best deer country. Concerning the deer's control, Sir Richard Dyke Acland, who left "Holnicote Estate" to the Trust, did so incorporating a Deed of Gift that hunting deer with hounds should always be permitted on this land.

So far, Exmoor's strong preservation attitude to deer for sport has been highlighted but other reasons for this preservation attitude also exist, one of which is tourism. Thousands come to Exmoor annually and the deer are an added attraction. Indeed many people holiday on Exmoor especially to watch and photograph deer, partly because of their rarity in the wild in England. Many farmers and landowners augment their income from tourism ie. campsites, holiday cottages and farmhouse accommodation, giving many an added incentive to preserve the attraction of the existence of wild deer. In support of Exmoor's deer, it has to be questioned what has been done for them in return for what they have done for Exmoor. Opposition to blood sports has also benefited Exmoor's wild deer. The League Against Cruel Sports have purchased a number of sanctuary areas open to the range of deer which are important havens and strongholds.

At the centre of a considerable conflict over reasons to preserve them, exists a sizeable population of wild Red deer within the area of the Exmoor National Park and beyond its boundaries. Despite a

The Devon and Somerset Staghounds.

level of preservation which has resulted in their survival to the present day, there is another darker side which is the number of deer that are shot quite legally, some of which are sold to game dealers and in some cases the shooters are also dealers. Some of the shooting of deer on Exmoor is carried out within management plans by such landowners as the National Trust and the Forestry Commission on land under their ownership which is on the fringe of hunting districts and places where the staghounds rarely visit. Despite all the preservation afforded to the wild Red deer of Exmoor they have never been and are not immune to the actions of some landowners who have no wish to allow any deer to range over their land and they either personally shoot or permit others to do so, with considerable financial gain to be had, until the deer are a rarity on that ground. Little is heard of this as the media home in on the headline news of hunting with hound incidents and all shooting losses are said to be the result of illegal poaching activities. Numbers taken by the opportunist illegal poachers are quite insignificant in comparison to the uncontrolled legal shooting of deer and selling, which can wipe out whole areas completely and where one landowner of a small acreage adopts such a policy, can be a constant danger to neighbours trying to preserve the animal.

To those concerned for the deer and putting aside the hunting with hounds controversy, what is most alarming is the lack of control over all hunting activities, most especially hunting with the gun. No limits are set over how many a year a person can take and a person can obtain a licence to shoot, with relative ease once the permission of a landowner has been obtained. The very fact that no one can confidently say exactly how many wild Red deer are killed annually on Exmoor calls for urgent legislation to control this situation. The following two chapters cover the two methods of deer control practised on Exmoor — that with horse and hound (Hunting of Deer on Exmoor) and that with the gun (Shooting Deer on Exmoor).

HUNTING OF DEER ON EXMOOR

Three packs of staghounds are operative in the West Country of England, The Devon and Somerset Staghounds (D. & S.), The Tiverton Staghounds and The Quantock Staghounds. Each hunt in and around their respective districts on land where the sporting rights are held by the hunt or on private land where the hunt are permitted. The D. & S. Staghounds' operations are almost entirely confined to the district of Exmoor with their kennels at Exford in the middle of the National Park. The pack consists of approximately forty five couple of hounds and the hunt has a full time hunting, kennel and stable staff. The whole operation of the hunt is self-financed with income from subscriptions, also "Cap" — the collection made at every meet from all followers of the hunt and there are numerous annual fundraising events. The Master or Masters of the Hunt, as is today appropriate accept their post by guaranteeing an annual sum.

The hunting season is from early August until the end of April. The season commences with the traditional opening meet at Cloutsham Farm in the Horner district of Exmoor on the second Saturday in August. The Hunt will have already been out on three or four days prior to this on what is termed as Bye Days. Barring sickness to horses or hounds or periods of winter weather that renders hunting impossible the D. & S. hunt three days a week regularly throughout the season, usually on Tuesdays, Thursdays and Saturdays. From the commencement of hunting in August until the end of October mature stags are the quarry of the hunt and this is known as autumn staghunting. Then after a short break the hind hunting season begins in early November until the end of February when attention is then focused on the hunting of spring stags, (three to four year olds) until the end of April and the finish of the hunting season.

Today the D. & S. Staghounds are accounting for approximately a hundred deer annually, made up of an average 20 autumn stags, 12 spring stags and around 60 hinds. Some do include injured deer, the result of gunshot wounds, injuries on wire fences especially barbed wire and some road casualties. Thankfully the hunt will always follow up reports of such deer and make every effort to find and put them out of their misery. On occasions during the close season for hunting the hunt marksman has to be called upon to deal with a casualty.

Hunted stag in the Exe Valley.

The D. & S. Staghounds continue to conduct their operations in the time honoured tradition of the moor, the sport remaining ever popular, most importantly amongst the hunt-supporting farmers and landowners for, without their co-operation the hunting would not last another day and the wide range of the deer would be further threatened.

Many books have been written in the past concerning the hunting of deer on Exmoor. One classic was written by a Hunt Harbourer, the person appointed by the hunt, whose job it is to locate the whereabouts of a suitably aged stag to hunt. The book was "Memoirs of a Stag Harbourer" by Fred Goss, who harboured for the D. & S. Staghounds from 1894 to 1921 under seven masters harbouring over 1,200 stags.

For me this book depicts the heyday of hunting of wild Red deer on Exmoor. The country where Goss practised his woodcraft was still relatively untamed and undisturbed. The motor car was still in its infancy and what roads existed were but rough pony tracks. Goss covered the whole district alone on horseback and he would ride to the district to be hunted the day prior to the meet, after harbouring that evening, stay overnight at a local farm, to be out again at first light the following morning. The study of heads taken by the hunt during Goss's harbouring era, which can still be found hanging in buildings and porches all over Exmoor, are testament to the finer quality of Exmoor's deer in those olden days compared to today. One reason why was that shooting of deer was much more of a crime. Without ease of transport and freezers, poaching and shooting for the pot was naturally restricted and with less pressure on the deer, stags were more plentiful, living longer, so growing bigger.

On average much greater distances were covered by the hunt in those olden days as the country lent itself much more to a free run for the deer and hounds without today's web of wire fencing and roads lined with motor cars. None of these problems as well as the fact that hardly a voice of opposition was raised against blood sports. Adding it all up one can but admire the dedication of the modern day hunting fraternity on Exmoor who strive to see the continuation of their sport in the wake of such difficult circumstances and in some areas alone keep the dimmed light of the candle burning for the deer that they so love to hunt.

As in the past preparation for a modern day autumn stag hunting begins the evening prior to the meet when the work of harbouring a suitable stag begins. Today the hunt have two official harbourers who share the country and do most of their work with the aid of

Big four a top stag roused from his lying bed.

vehicle. The harbourers of today, like Goss, rely on the goodwill of hunt-supporting farmers who can usually greatly assist with detailed information of the whereabouts of deer which they will have regularly seen whilst about their work on the land. Obviously not any stag will do. For autumn staghunting it is rare for the hunt to kill a stag less than a brow trey two a-top or four to five year old and this is usually when an older more warrantable stag could not be found.

When the opportunity arises attention is focused on the hunting of ideal cull stags such as ones old and going back, knott stags, one antlered stags and any sick or wounded. Despite this, just as often the deer that is taken by the hunt can be perfectly fit and healthy. On such an occasion, especially in the case of a good stag from a district where in this day and age their occurrence can be far too rare, it can be extremely regrettable.

As the time of the advertised meet of the staghounds approaches, so sees the arrival of supporters and avid followers of hunting. It is a red letter day for local folk, very much a social event in the district and there is that atmosphere of camaraderie with little class distinction between the mounted followers and as it is today, the majority on a popular day, that are mechanically propelled. Depending on the distance from the kennels at Exford, the hounds are either boxed or walked to the meet. Of those that are mounted at the meet, only the huntsmen, the whip and gentlemen masters of hounds can wear the scarlet hunting jacket. As they stand and parade with the hounds against a back-drop of the sweeping Exmoor country, they make a splendid old English sight especially for the countless visitors attracted to the spectacle of this ancient Exmoor custom.

A large breed of hound is used for stag hunting and the hunt use either the dog or the bitch pack but never hunt them together; they are always counted in couples. One of the attributes of a good huntsman, is that he knows and loves his hounds. Any person's conception of hunting deer on Exmoor as being that of a band of totally disorganised rustics in charge of a fierce pack of wild dogs with which they course and savage any unfortunate deer is quite misinformed as to the traditional ways of staghunting. The hounds are so fierce and uncontrolled that the hunt have the confidence to permit the public, including children, to approach and mingle amidst the hounds at the meet. The hunting of the deer is conducted by adhering to the ancient rules of the art of venery.

While the meet is in progress, the harbourer reports to the masters of the whereabouts of one or more suitable stags to hunt. On the information received a decision is made as to where the hounds will be taken to draw (find a stag). With the formalities over, a move is made and the master announces "Hounds, Gentlemen Please" and with a blow from the huntsman's horn, the hounds are immediately boxed. The huntsman then proceeds to pick out seven or eight couple of his most seasoned of hounds, these few hounds are called the tufters and are used for the initial search for the suitable stag. This operation is described as tufting.

The tufting operation can take anything from a few minutes if the deer is harboured to the inch, or can take several hours of painstakingly drawing and returning to large woodland covers when a suitable stag is difficult to find and persuade to break cover. Only on the rare occasion when a harboured stag is known to be lying on his own is tufting dispensed with and the main pack is used to rouse the deer.

Before the harbourer proceeds to lead the huntsman and his tufters to where the stag is harboured a few experienced mounted followers are sent to strategic positions to act as a lookout for the stag while the "field", the main body of the mounted followers wait together for the start of the hunt proper, under the control of a field master. In these modern times, it is the cars and landrovers and motorcycles that make the most impact. Every accessible road and track surrounding the place where the stag is harboured is likely to be jammed solid, sadly often diminishing the chance of the hunted deer making an uninterrupted break from cover.

The huntsman begins to encourage his tufters to find the stag with short notes on his horn. In hunting circles, the sound of hounds that have viewed or scented a deer is described as anything but barking. They can be speaking, crying, giving tongue and the sound of a pack in unison is often described as music. It is indeed music to the ears of followers to hear the tufters for it is a sure sign that a deer or some deer are on foot.

All spectators are now hoping to see deer break cover and on the move. Seasoned followers that know the wild Red deer, play a major role here, by assessing the deer and either signalling that it is a warrantable stag to hunt or be prepared to assist in stopping the tufters off unsuitables. A loud holler, the blowing of a whistle or the wave of a white handkerchief are all signals that a person might use should they have viewed a warrantable stag. Often acting on these signals or messages received the huntsman might well stop his tufters off another line and lift (take) them to where the stag has been viewed. On occasions, the hounds may run the line of a deer in the wrong direction, which is known as running heel line, when they will also be stopped.

Whilst the tufters are being held up, a messenger is sent to signal that the main pack is requested by the master. The time spent holding up the tufters and waiting for the pack is known as "law" or time of grace given to the stag to get a head start. In olden times it was certainly considered unsporting, if not a crime, for any person to track the route of the hunted stag during the time of law. Today it is common for streams of mechanically propelled followers to head off in the direction of the stag during the time of law and in recent years, I have seen riders to gallop after the stag and attempt to turn him in a favourable direction for the hunt.

And so the laying on of the pack signals the start of the hunting run and the field of mounted followers join in. Great distances can be covered and therefore during any hunt the huntsman, the whip and the masters all have a change of horse available. It is the unenviable task of the second horse lads or apprentices to have the fresh horses they are riding at hand at the right place and time, anticipating short cuts so not tiring the fresh horse before the change.

All manner of factors contribute to the run of the hunted stag and the great distance that may or may not be covered. Stags that are hunted early in the season are carrying excess fat and seldom run far but twist and turn and are loath to leave the area where they have been living all summer. Stags that are hunted at the end of the season have already been rendered in poor condition from the rigours and excursions of rutting activity, even before they may be hunted. As well as the condition of the quarry, the amount of scent it is leaving for the hounds to follow also has a great bearing on a day's hunting, for it varies considerably from day to day. Scent can be almost non-existent during dry conditions especially early in the season when the deer are yet to acquire their musty autumnal odours. Day after day can pass with little of note being done by the hounds.

It is in no way a certainty that once the hounds settle onto the line of a stag that his death is inevitable, neither is it certain that in the event of a kill that it is always the stag that was carefully selected by the harbourer in the morning. The Red deer possess great fleetness of foot, stamina and with age they learn great cunning. One common ploy is for a hunted deer to constantly join a fresh herd. An old stag will beat the covers if being hunted, looking for a substitute to transfer the burden upon of being pursued. For this reason, a hunted deer is most likely to run into the wind in open country hoping to scent other deer. It is the ploy of deer that are not being hunted to stand motionless, often extremely close to the hounds that are on the line of other deer, so they might avoid being viewed.

A deer lying tight, say an old stag in high cover, will often not attempt to move until the last possible moment when he knows the hounds are on to him.

Once more, hunt followers in vehicles have a great bearing on the course of the hunt for many do not follow the run of the hounds but are constantly trying to get ahead of the hunted stag. Therefore it is a rare modern staghunting day when the hounds are not lifted considerable distances forward to someone's signal. How often a well run up stag, that has fairly and squarely shaken off the hounds is then unsportingly betrayed by someone, and it only needs one person to see the stag, pass on the information and instigate a kill.

Water figures a great deal in the hunting of the wild Red deer. Many hunted deer have often run the course of a river to eventually leave it again having masked their scent. On occasions some submerge themselves in a deep pool of a river, with just their nose above the water and there remain until it is safe.

On the coast, throughout the history of staghunting on Exmoor, hunted deer have readily taken to swimming out to sea. Though excellent swimmers deer are unable to exhale any intake of water and too long in the sea, especially when conditions are bad, will lead to drowning. The majority of hunted deer that are brought to bay by the hunt take to water, usually a river or stream, though some seek somewhere inaccessible such as high up on a cliff. Some seek the shelter of buildings or jump onto lean-to roofs. If a hunted deer fails to reach any of the fore-mentioned places it may simply stand in the middle or corner of a garden or field or sometimes right out on the open moor.

It is always the intention of the hunt to dispatch the deer that fail in their bid to outrun and outwit them, with the gun. Either by holding the deer, enabling a dispatch with a humane killer to the head, the huntsman always carries such a weapon, or the deer may be shot at close range using a shotgun loaded with permissible cartridge for deer; the hunt appoint a couple of mounted followers experienced in the run of the deer and good marksmen with the gun.

Stag at bay high up on the cliffs.

Gone to sea.

69

Having witnessed countless hunt kills, I would state that the degree of cruelty varies from one hunt kill to another. All are subjected to the chase and many are brought to a pitiful state of exhaustion. For some, when their strength is failing, a state of panic sets in and the deer's actions become irrational and many wound themselves, crashing blindly through wire fences and undergrowth before they are eventually killed.

It is not my wish to give explicit personal accounts of the runs and harrowing ends that have been met by some Red deer at the hands of the hunt for sport. They are a regular occurrence like the proportion of kills that can be swift and relatively humane. There are a number of obvious factors that can contribute to this degree of cruelty which are as follows:-

1. What is the physical condition that the rigours of the chase have rendered the animal.

2. In the time that often passes before the hunt gun arrives on the scene, what is the mental trauma of a deer confronted by a pack of hounds and a crowd before it is eventually shot.

3. If the hunted deer and the hounds are out of touch of people, are all deer capable of keeping hounds at bay. In most instances only stags with the weaponry of antlers are.

4. What is the size and conduct of the adrenalin-charged hunt crowd that has gathered to be in at a kill, with the live exhausted hunted deer at hand.

5. What is the physical state of the person appointed to carry a gun when he is called upon to use it. Is he always calm and collected to dispatch the deer cleanly with one shot or is he out of breath and shaking, increasing the chance of more than one shot required.

Whatever the degree of cruelty to the deer, there is no excuse for it. It is not born out of poverty and hunger. Man should and does know different. In the case put forward by those who support staghunting the back-bone of their argument is the certain withdrawal of an existence given to the wild Red deer by hunt-supporting Exmoor landowners, should they be deprived of their favourite pastime. This is not some empty threat but the reality of the situation. The best part of Exmoor's wild Red deer could be quite legally eradicated as a pest from areas where at present they are tolerated to a certain degree. Controlled use of the gun is the most effective method of culling deer known to man but without the control then a popular blood sport's existence is the most effective method of deer preservation in the absence of legislative control. None of this makes hunting deer with hounds correct but serves to epitomise man's inhumanity to animals in a civilized country.

Great ceremony follows any hunt kill where the huntsman publicly opens up the deer; traditionally the liver is sliced and handed out to the followers. The heart, when appropriate is given to the owner of the land where the deer was taken. The huntsman removes the slots (feet) of the deer which as his property he will offer for sale to those wanting a trophy and reminder of the day's sport. Back teeth are often removed for tie pins, some people might pull out a small clump of neck hair to put on a hat. Eventually the carcass is lifted away and hounds receive their eagerly awaited reward of the remaining entrails. If requested, young followers in at their first kill could be blooded with a cross on the forehead by the huntsman, a ritual I am not certain still takes place.

The carcass is taken away to be later skinned and butchered into joints which are distributed to farmers and landowners over whose land the deer ran. The joint of venison is sent with a note from the masters conveying their compliments. In the case of a stag the most prized possession is the head of antlers and with the bones for the hounds it is returned to the kennels. Only in the case of an exceptional trophy will the whole head and antlers be treated by a taxidermist. Normally the head is boiled out and the skull is cut so that it can be mounted on a plaque stating where it was found and where killed (taken). All of the stag's heads are the possession of the current master or masters of the hunt.

The autumn stag hunting season finishes at the end of October when normally there is a short break of a week or two before the commencement of the hind hunting season. Unlike stag hunting, the abundance of the female Red deer population does not necessitate any complicated harbouring operations. A discussion at the meet amongst landowners and farmers will usually suffice to ascertain the whereabouts of hinds to hunt, indeed it is a rare meet on the open moor when deer cannot be viewed from the venue. With the ending of organised hunt deer drives, to cull hinds, early in the 1980's, today the hunt hind cull is invariably left wanting. More hind hunting days are postponed due to fog, gales and snow than at any other time and there is a higher degree of difficulty in accounting for an adequate number of hinds by hunting them using the same method adopted for stags. An old hind possesses superior stamina and cunning with the advantage of not carrying the extra burden of a pair of antlers, which for stags also makes it easier for hunt followers to distinguish the hunted deer from others, so regularly putting the hounds back on the right track. There is less such assistance forthcoming from fewer followers who attend the less popular hind hunting days.

The hind hunting season finishes at the end of February and spring stag hunting begins immediately, when the hunt resort back to harbouring their quarry again. The main difference between autumn and spring stag hunting is the age and experience of the stag. A hunted spring stag is far more likely to simply try and outrun the hounds without using any cunning ploys and have and do regularly give the hunt long runs and good sport.

The end of April sees the finish of the spring stag hunting and the finish of the hunting season. For just over three months there is a summer close season when hinds are calving and stags are regrowing their antlers. The main hunt event during the close season is the annual Puppy Show which is held in July. The hunt farm out young hound puppies to numerous hunt supporters who rear them and train them before they are ready for their first hunting season. This is known as puppy walking and at the Puppy Show all these young hounds are judged. Another attraction at this show is the display of all the heads of the stags taken during the last hunting season. As owners of them, the masters are entitled to present them to hunt-supporting farmers and landowners within the hunting district. Some are presented for prizes at Point To Point Horse Races and at Horse Shows and also for retirement gifts. However, many stags' heads are permanently retained at the hunt kennels.

Such has been the merest sketch of the ways of the sport that is conducted on Exmoor, which most importantly is the major incentive of private landowners to preserve the wild Red deer.

DEER SHOOTING ON EXMOOR

The gun is a lethal killing machine which gives man the power to conserve or destroy the wild Red deer of Exmoor. The existence of the sport of hunting deer with hounds and its popularity has controlled this power over the centuries with deer preserved for the sport.

Hunting alone proved to be an inadequate method of deer control but a good method of conservation. During the war years this was best highlighted. With the drive for agriculture, the number of deer throughout the Exmoor district was unacceptable and had to be reduced. Numbers were reduced by organised deer drives on order of the "War Agricultural Committee". On these drives the hunt used a few hounds to move the deer to waiting individuals with shot-guns.

And so began a long period of stability. The war ended but the practice of deer drives organised by the hunt continued. The guns used were shotguns, using SSG shot in the hands of men appointed by the hunt, usually local farmers. This method continued to prove to be extremely effective.

The large number of deer taken out through this method could easily be passed off as being taken by hunting, even though it was nothing more than a deer shoot. Another enormous benefit was that this shooting preserved stags as it was in the interest of stag hunting to leave them for future hunting days. Mainly hinds were taken to reduce the deer population and the balance of the sexes was maintained.

This system of deer management was wrecked in 1981 by an Act of Parliament, "The Wildlife and Countryside Act" which saw to the abolition of the shotgun as a general legal weapon for deer and also made it illegal to drive deer to the gun. At this time it might have seemed a simple matter for the hunt to change from deer drives to marksmen with high powered rifles, the now legal weapon, and undertake deer control on Exmoor. Sadly no such change was forthcoming. Covering up the necessity to shoot was easy with deer drives but organising shooting with no need for the huntsman and his hounds would obviously not have looked good for stag hunting. Many hunting people had always maintained it impossible to shoot deer on Exmoor.

Many landowners had depended on the deer drives.

Uncoordinated individual action had always been uncommon. Through the 1980's the rifle began to be used extensively under no controls or management system. The owner of land with hunting rights can obtain a rifle or give written permission to others with the appropriate gun licence to take deer on their land. Sadly some areas were completely cleared of Red deer in a few short years. Unlike in the past much of the shooting was unselective and profit motivated. Heavy deer such as mature stags were given no grace now. Wounding of deer

Mature stags began to become rarer through the 1980's.

was also on the increase.

During the mid 1980's it was estimated that in excess of twenty game dealers were operating and collecting deer from the West Country. As these dealers are registered in the areas where they come from and not from where they collect, exact information on numbers taken is unknown. Also the number of licensed individuals in possession of rifles throughout the West Country is veiled in secrecy. One clue was the result of an official study at the time that was looking into the public hygiene implications of this sudden influx of venison reaching the food chain.

Part of the study involved the police and environmental health officers examining game dealers' records which indicated at the time that in excess of one thousand Red deer had been taken from the Exmoor district in one year. This was indeed a sad period as now the deer were being hunted and shot. No longer were the two working in harmony.

Coming under pressure now there was also a noticeable change in the deer's distribution. Conservation areas such as National Trust and League Against Cruel Sports sanctuaries saw considerable increases in numbers, hind numbers, especially as their number were no longer kept in check by deer drives. Increases in these certain areas tended to offset the losses elsewhere.

It is clear that the situation concerning the shooting of deer within and around the Exmoor district is far from a satisfactory one.

Officially some deer are taken through hunting, and some are taken by stalkers appointed by The National Trust and Forestry Commission. In reality the deer are shot annually by all and sundry, and all too often treated as a pest. Urgent legislation is needed to introduce a system where all shooting of Red deer in the West Country is part of an overall management system, which sees to fair treatment of the animal and where preservation of the species is the priority.

STAG HORNING

With the arrival of spring, one by one the stags shed their antlers. They may drop them in the woods or on the moor where they were spending the day or in the fields where they were feeding at night. On Exmoor "stag horning" describes the pastime of searching for these highly prized objects. In each district one will find those few people who take this pastime seriously and are prepared to walk many miles and devote many hours in search of them. Those that are regularly successful, obviously have a good knowledge of the deer, the country they inhabit, and follow up the stags closely before

the dropping season. Despite this a few are found every year just by chance by the casual walker. The find can be a great thrill especially if one should be lucky enough to find a big pair lying together or a little way apart. Even more satisfying if they are from a well known stag that has been observed and photographed throughout the last deer watching year. Compared to Deer Parks, the chances of finding the antlers in the wild are very slender and they are likely to be smaller but it is the challenge of finding a fine pair from the truly wild Red stag living in his natural state that spurs the searcher on.

A stag I called Lobster Tops. A few weeks after this picture was taken I was thrilled to find his antlers.

76

When mounted professionally a shed pair can look just, if not more, attractive than any shooting or hunting trophy on a skull. Also with the shed antlers there is also the added satisfaction of knowing that he lived on.

The older the stag the earlier his shedding date is likely to be. A good friend of mine "Mr Carl Clarke" of Minehead, found a fine four a-top antler on the 11th March on North Hill, the earliest I have known. As the shedding season approaches it is obviously a great advantage to know the whereabouts of

The Author surrounded by some of the antlers he has found. Pieces of old friends.

the stags in the district and strive to observe them regularly, without disturbing them throughout the antler dropping time.

A stag is well aware that his antlers are near to shedding and takes every precaution possible to stall the event. He carries his head carefully, more erect and rigid than normal and the last thing he will do is to purposely knock them off. Feeding carries on normally and a fine field of favoured young grass can be enough to hold a stag herd in an area while they are shedding antlers. The unavoidable jump in and out of the field is a very likely place for a stag to drop his antlers or anywhere else where the stags have to jump and jolt their heads.

Occasionally, it is possible to observe the top of the pedicles of a stag that has recently cast his antlers. If the layer appears red and raw - only a short period of time has passed since he shed. If it appears blue and bruised, two days may have passed in which time he could have travelled some distance and his antlers could be a long way away.

It is quite common for a stag to shed his antlers simultaneously especially in the case of older, heavier stags. If not together, a heavy antlered stag will probably shed them quite close together. Once he has shed one antler and is left suddenly lop-sided, by shaking his head and sometimes jumping repeatedly up and down he will rid himself of the second antler and drop it in a short time. So, should one be fortunate enough to find one antler it is always the best policy to begin one's search for the fellow by looking in the immediate vicinity. Inevitably, the two antlers of a pair are found by different people. This can lead to much haggling over which party would be prepared to part with and sell their treasured find.

On 29th March, 1997 I had settled down one afternoon to watch seven stags browsing peacefully down through the trees of a steep wooded valley side. They had been resident there for some time and I was hoping in the next few weeks to find their antlers. Amongst them there was a very fine 4-3 a-top and also a stag with an old head going back. Suddenly for no apparent reason, something frightened them and they took off through the wood. I was puzzled, as there was no one down there and there seemed no reason for their sudden fright. I found them again a short distance away and it was then when I noticed the old stag had shed. The reason for their unexpected fright then dawned on me. I went back to the spot where it had happened and sure enough there was his antlers lying one on top of the other. I hadn't seen it but while I was there the clatter of his antlers as they fell to the ground had caused the stags to take off in fright.

I observed a similar but quite unique incident on the 17th March 1988 out on the open moorland. This time I was watching a large herd of twenty stags and from binocular distance one morning, I settled down in the heather to enjoy the spectacle. Again there were some fine stags amongst them, one was an outstanding two a-top. They were passing a favoured soiling pit at the head of a coombe. Many of them stopped to soil and the herd became separated. It was a fine sight to watch them all emerging black and sodden. As is common-place, many stags reflect their enjoyment and refreshment afterwards in some boisterous behaviour. Suddenly one large stag lunged at the master two a-top who met this potential threat to his supremacy head on. Though some distance away, I heard what must have been a mighty clash of antlers quite clearly. To my astonishment, the master stag came out of it minus his antlers and sloped away naked. The challenger seemed somewhat surprised, left circling what was left of his opponent, a pair of antlers on the ground. By this time I was not really sure that what I had just witnessed had really happened. Making my way over to the spot, my heart was racing with excitement. Seeing them and picking up the splendid pair that only minutes before were being carried by the stag was a little too much to take in. On the triumphant trek home, my good fortune eventually did sink in. The sort of incident that a stag horner might only dream about.

There is always a great deal of friendly rivalry amongst local stag horners culminating at local shows where antler competitions are held and it is the annual get-together of stag horners who have plenty to tell and share their stories of successes and failures.

One local family the "Barwicks" of Hawkcombe were avid searchers. With their knowledge of the deer they often all went out together and working as a team they covered a great deal of ground and found countless numbers of antlers. In her later years the (late) Mrs Alice Barwick senior still, though very crippled, had her enthusiasm for the pursuit. She could no longer follow the rest of her family and so she stayed around the starting point as the rest went off in the woods. While waiting for their return she slowly struggled up over the side to reach the field hedge a few hundred yards away. There, under the fence where a stag had passed that night, she found the most splendid three a-top pair while the others returned with nothing that day.

A chapter on finding antlers on Exmoor would not be complete without mentioning my old friend Mr Ted Davey of Brompton Regis. Ted's knowledge of the deer and his beloved Haddon District is unparalleled. He has a remarkably large collection of shed antlers with a story to tell you attached to each of them. He gives pride of place to a white and weathered brow trey and six a-top antler. The story attached to it is fascinating. One summer's afternoon he took a break from his work in the fields and sought the cool of the wood for a walk. He had not been far when he noticed the point of a stag's antler protruding from the foot of a holly tree. He at first thought it just a small one and went to pick it out. Much tugging would not move it and he had to return with tools to dig it out. The holly tree had grown over it and it was entangled in its roots. This remarkable antler must have been there for years. Ted was not satisfied until he had found out the history of the great master stag that must have shed it. At Miss Abbot's (Master of Staghounds) at Dulverton he eventually found the head of this unmistakable stag which had been killed twenty years previous to Ted finding one of his shed antlers. From this story it is further evidence of the fact that in the West Country shed antlers can resist the attacks of nature for many years. Who knows what other secrets the woods are hiding.

Seldom do I leave Exmoor but an invitation to some friends at 'Kenton" near Exeter, Mr & Mrs Ted Crowther, and a weekend of searching for the elusive Red deer on Dartmoor lured me away one weekend in the winter of 1987. Arriving in suburbia, a small garden on a housing estate seemed the last place to find an antler but to the astonishment of everyone, myself included, under a bush I found a Roe buck's antler which had probably been carried there by a dog. The next day on the Dartmoor trek and my first visit, I came out of the woods with a fine brow trey two a-top antler. My bemused hosts jokingly vowed to never invite me again.

SOME FAVOURITE STAGS

I have fond memories of many Exmoor stags. Each one had his own individuality and different habits and it is impossible as a deer lover not to become attached to some of them. The following is an account of four Master Exmoor stags whose lives I studied and who gave me countless hours of pleasure. The first one was known as "Clump Head".

"Clump Head"

I would estimate that Clump Head was born around the mid 1960's. His country was the Porlock covers and cliffs and the Culbone district. His likely birthplace would have been on Culbone Hill where he grew up, then in his adolescence he sought to break into the stag herd of the Porlock coverts. Clump Head was recognisable by his exceptionally long antlers, with long brow points, never possessing a bay point, then trey and top points. He acquired his nickname after one year when his top points failed to develop and he was left with clumpy tops. From then on he was unmistakable though his clumpy tops improved again after better summers and he grew some very fine heads with long top points.

Clump Head on the right as the stags make their way up through Westcott Brake

For nearly ten years I knew him and he was more than any other stag, part of the furniture of the woods.

While he was growing his antlers in summer, he had three favourite lying beds where you could almost guarantee to go and find him at home. At this time of the year he preferred to be alone. One of his favourite lying places was in a ferry brake under a farm. From the other side of the valley one could look across to see his velvet antlers just showing above the ferns as he lay there enjoying the warmth and sunshine and listening to the comings and goings of the farm and the monotonous stroke of the farm generator. If he wasn't there, another of his daytime lying places was in the bushes at the back of a quarry by a busy road. Visitors would often stop for a picnic then leave without knowing about Clump Head's presence. Clump Head would also seek the quiet and solitude of the woods on Furnace Knap above Porlock Weir.

Though reasonably tolerant of people the slightest sign of the presence of the hunt and sound of speaking hounds and Clump Head was gone. With not a moment to lose he headed for the cliffs and disappeared for a few days until the coast was clear again. He had long established himself as the master stag in the Culbone district during the rut and year after year he made his rutting stand on "Stent Hill". After the rut he sought again his woodland wintering quarters in the Porlock coverts and gathered all the local stags together to lead them throughout the winter. He regularly took them for nightly feeding raids down in the fields in the Porlock Vale and on one special day, they stayed on the Porlock Marshes in full view of everyone all day.

During his lifetime Clump Head shed some very fine antlers, some of which I was lucky enough to find. On one occasion during antler dropping time I was travelling the road from Porlock to Porlock Weir. We had had heavy rain and just past "West Porlock" I noticed a muddy trail across the tarmac road. I immediately stopped as it was obviously the place where Clump Head's herd of stags had crossed that night. As I peered over the rack in the hedge my eyes lit up as I could see both of Clump Head's antlers at the foot of the drop into the field the other side.

Unbeknown to me, this fine pair were to be the last antlers he was ever to shed. It was inevitable that he could not go on evading the hunt for ever. Old Clump Head had been the greatest campaigner I had known but his regular rutting habits were eventually to be his downfall. It was the rut of 1978 and sure enough Clump Head was back on Stent Hill. He was then probably around 15 years old but still carrying a vigorous head. It was not the first time he had been harboured for the hunt or the one that they had chosen to pursue. On that particular day it turned out that Clump Head was their second string for the tufters spent the first part of the day in the Parks searching for another big stag. They could not settle onto him and so as Clump Head had been seen, hounds were lifted and brought to "Stent Hill". No sooner than they were put into the cover, Clump Head was jumping the fence the other side and taking the most direct route down over the fields at Silcombe and into the cliff country which had been his saviour so many times before. This time the hounds were close behind him and he was pushed into going to sea at Foreland Point. Later that day I heard the news of his death. He had been shot as he returned to the beach. For a long time after his passing the woods were very empty without him around.

"Big George"

Few West Country stags achieve the sort of antler growth that was carried by an Exe Valley stag that was known as "Big George". He spent his whole life in the various woodlands in the Exe Valley and like all the stags of that district benefited from the availability of rich farmland feeding. But Big George was so exceptional that it was a privilege to witness such a sight. He grew his best head throughout the summer of 1983 with his usual mighty spread with great long rights and a splendid three a-top.

I was fortunate that summer, to be able to gradually watch this outstanding head develop week by week. The first sighting of the summer was in May. So advanced was his antler growth that he had at least a foot more than his nearest rival in that splendid herd of sixteen stags. He was probably around twelve years old and he made a splendid leader for the herd. He was extremely alert and difficult to outwit. No doubt this was the main reason why he had lived so long and grown so big. Never had I been so determined to capture something on film than I was to record the sight of this quite unique stag in his prime and one of the largest wild Exmoor stags I had ever seen.

It was mid-July. The days were hot and dry. Big George's stag herd had been spending the days lately lying in the cool of a thick fir plantation adjoining lush fields of grass. Every night they would

Big George was the first to look up.

cautiously come out of the wood to feed. One evening I decided to lay in wait for them, flat on my stomach in the middle of the field. After about an hour my patience was almost exhausted and I was becoming uncomfortable when at last I heard the unmistakable cracking of branches and movement in the wood. They were starting to come out to feed.

Though it was late, there was still enough light to film. One by one they came over the hedge. Big George paused on the top for a while, sniffed the air then jumped down to join the others. He was unsettled and had probably just caught the hint of my scent but did not realise I was only a short distance from them. Closer and closer they came, the tension was becoming unbearable. I had to make my move so while I was sure each one had his head down feeding I raised the camera and got myself comfortable to take. Then I waited for my moment. The time was right. The first shot was with them all feeding, Big George was the first to look up *(see above)*. Another shot and they were off, it was all over in a few seconds and I was left with that marvellous sense of achievement while making my way home that night.

A few weeks later and all the stags had left their summering quarters to travel away to rut. Big George made his rutting stand in the L.A.C.S. sanctuary at Baronsdown near Dulverton. It was another safe place to be and obviously another reason for his great longevity. That foggy morning in October when I observed him he had a harem of over 40 hinds. He was crazy with the fever of the rut, his balve echoing across the valley and he was making frenzied attacks to the ground sending great clods of turf flying into the air. Big George remained unrivalled that rut.

In January 1984 normality was returning to the deer herds and stags were gathering up again and re-forming the bachelor herd in the Exe. I had accounted for most of them except Big George. At first I was not perturbed as I just thought he was still around but lying low, but as the weeks went by and there was still no sign of him, alarm bells began to ring amongst the local deer fraternity. Nobody had seen Big George and rumours began to filter through that he had been shot. The victim of a trophy hunter's gun. Still I continued the search not wanting to believe it, but now long after those happier days and the memory of Big George, I am certain that that was what became of him. A sad end to one of the Kings of Exmoor Stags.

"Rooster"

Rooster was the King of the Exmoor Forest. His heartland was this expanse of grass and heather moor where the forest herd of stags that Rooster belonged to roamed. He came up through the ranks of this herd during the 1970's and it was well known in the district that an exceptional stag that stood out from the rest was at large though when it came to hunting, Rooster was extremely cunning. He'd learnt his forest home well from the bleak molinia moors of Pinford and Buscombe to the heather clad hills of Mill Hill. When being hunted Rooster had mastered the art of vanishing without trace. One of his favourite ploys was to run weir water, masking his scent, then he would leave the water and climb out to lie up in a place of cover.

Rooster would travel into the Dunkery district for the rut. In the rut of 1979 he only came as far as the Nutscale district where he held his harem in the maze of deep coombes in that area. He looked proud on the skyline with his characteristic great beam of antler and that year he carried all his rights and three a-top both sides. The following spring I took up the challenge of finding him in the hope of picking up his antlers .

For many weeks I could not find him, which rather dashed my hopes. The forest was thousands of acres of moorland and to look

Rooster and his herd crossing Chalk Water (1981)

for his antlers with no knowledge of his whereabouts was like looking for a needle in a haystack. After a long disappearance he suddenly turned up again and joined the Buscombe herd out in the middle of the forest. For such a large stag I expected him to shed around late March, beginning of April and I devoted all my efforts to keeping an eye on him every day. By the second week in April I was beginning to wonder if they were ever going to come off. It was a four mile walk to where they were lying, to often return satisfied that he was still carrying them. Even if I did see that he had shed, it was still a slim, daunting task to begin the search as they often roamed miles at night to feed.

On the second Thursday of April 1980, it was a fine morning and I spied them out on the hill. They were restless and after a while began to move off. Rooster was there proudly carrying his head. I watched them disappearing into the coombe and waited for them to emerge up the other side. As they all came in view again I could hardly believe my eyes. Rooster was shaking his head in shock, he had just lost both antlers. Down in the coombe amongst the rushes where they had just jumped the stream lay the antlers. I could hardly contain my feelings and quite out of keeping with a deer man, I hollered a mighty yell of joy.

Rooster with a few of his harem on Ley Hill, Horner District. October 1981.

It was as fine a pair of antlers as ever one could wish to find but unbeknown to me at the time Rooster was to go on to grow an even greater head. The following spring I heard that a farmer had found a big pair of antlers near Simonsbath. On investigation it turned out to be Rooster, who I had thought had disappeared.

During the 1981 rut Rooster appeared in the Horner district with a head of antlers the likes of which had not been seen on the hill for years. He carried a massive head with all his rights and four and three a-top *(see above)*. His antlers were extremely dark with a beam as big as a man's wrist. I recall one day hearing the tale of a hunting man who had seen Rooster in Horner Wood and described him as a stag who looked like he was carrying an oak tree on his head.

Rooster once again got through the rut unscathed but that winter he was to face a new danger in his forest winter haunt. The threat of being shot. The stags were often forced to come down off the hill to feed in neighbouring farmers' fields when times were hard. Unbeknown to them, one large landowner had turned against the deer and had given permission for a shooter to shoot the stags when they were seen on his land. Losses were heavy, at least 12 of the biggest forest stags were taken and Rooster was also missing.

The weeks passed, gradually the stags that remained learnt that there was another unsafe part of their range to be avoided. I had now convinced myself that Rooster was no more. That spring as a matter of respect to old Rooster, I decided to just go out to the spot where he had two years before run into the coombe and come out without his antlers

It was a lovely spring day. The forest was lit up in the sunshine. It was the same second Thursday in April and I had planned to reach the area at 10am. The visibility was so good that while stopping by the ruins at Larkbarrow to scan the country, my spirits were lifted at the sight of what I could make out to be stags away in the distance. This put an extra spring in my step and the long cross country trek to where they were lying did not seem so far.

Expecting to see just the usual stags that I knew were remaining, on closer inspection I could not believe my eyes. Old Rooster standing proudly amongst them after all that had happened (see top illustration, next page). He had somehow been clever enough to survive, I was overjoyed at the sight of him. After recovering from what was a great shock, I had almost forgotten what day it was, the day that I knew Rooster had shed his antlers in the past, and this was the exact spot where they had been lying two years before.

Then suddenly they caught my scent, I held my breath, were they going to enter the coombe? This time they made off in a different direction. I watched Rooster carefully, sure enough he was hanging back and holding his head rigid and careful and now the rest of the herd had already jumped a large dyke and were waiting for Rooster. He hesitated, then made his mind up to go. As he landed on the other side his right antler came off and fell to the ground. As he ran to join the other stags, he was frantically trying to rid himself of his other antler and his sudden lop-sided state (see bottom illustration, next page). Picking up this great antler, my concentration was intent on watching Rooster but now they had gone over the skyline. I ran to the top of the hill just in time to see the stags disappearing into the next big valley.

In the minute that they had been out of my sight Rooster had shed his other antler and so I knew where to search, as it had to be somewhere between where I was stood and where I had last seen them in the distance. I managed to find their slot marks and followed them on. Eventually I found the other antler and fell exhausted to the ground.

Old Rooster standing proudly amongst them.

As he ran to join the other stags, he was frantically trying to rid himself of his other antler.

On the same day at the same time it had happened again, a million to one chance, on top of the fact that when I woke up that day I didn't even think he was still alive. What an experience with deer - and one that I shall never forget.

Life went on for Rooster. He shed two more pairs though I was not to find any more of them. Right on cue in the rut of 1985, Rooster appeared in the Horner district. His head was now deteriorating and he was going back, though still he had the better of any other in the district. The rigours of that rut took their toll on Rooster and he was already weak and exhausted when he was hunted that October. After a short run in and around Horner Woods, Rooster never even attempted to make for his forest home. He was never to see it again for he stood gallantly to bay in Horner Water and was shot, at the end of a short hunt.

"Percy The Pet"

One stag I found most trusting of man was known as Percy The Pet. His characteristics suggested that as a calf he had been hand reared and re-introduced into the wild, though I have no knowledge of it. Though you could not touch him he would let you stand within a few feet as he grazed but not for everyone. It seemed that this privilege was only reserved for those whose scent and habits were known to him. To strangers in his wood he would be as wild and shy as any other stag, which made it difficult for those with the privilege to sound convincing. Any initial doubts about his health were not with grounds for he always looked well, had a fine two a-top pair of antlers and other than his trusting characteristic was quite normal. The person who gave him his name was an elderly lady, the late Mrs Harry Rawle of Porlock, who walked her dog every day along the same path that flanked Percy's wood. She too had gained the stag's trust.

Though Percy spent a lot of time alone he was not rejected by other deer. When he was in the company of other stags he showed none of his trusting temperament. Perhaps I will remember him the most for his liking for taking up residence in the paddock adjoining my cottage in summer. One corner of the paddock was overgrown with brambles and ferns, a favourite place for Percy where he could escape from the flies and heat of the woods in summer whilst his antlers were in velvet. Perhaps too, he enjoyed the view across Porlock Bay to Hurlestone Point. The local farmer whose fields Percy had regularly grazed, was a hunt supporter and in the traditional way of Exmoor this meant safety and security until the day when quarry was required for a day's sport. Up until now Percy had escaped detection which was somewhat due to the respect he had earned from his landlord. Percy was special and there was less co-operation forthcoming in betraying his presence.

The period when Percy was most vulnerable was during the rut, when he travelled away to gather up his harem of hinds. During previous years my interest in him had also led me many miles to locate where he rutted. I had long discovered that he had established himself as the master stag of a large hind herd that was resident in a maze of coombes in an area out on the open heather moor about five miles from his home territory. On one previous year Percy had been lucky to survive, for he was harboured and hunted but managed to find a way home and continued on around the coast and vanished into the remoteness of the rugged cliff country where the hunt lost him. Since that year, whenever the hunt was meeting for a stag-hunting day in the vicinity where Percy was rutting, I kept a watchful eye on the proceedings.

The years of Percy's long and charmed life were passing by. He was now carrying his most splendid head of antlers ever with all his rights and four and three a-top. The rut of the Red deer once more was upon us and one evening amongst the loyal band of deer watchers on the moor, who were marvelling at Percy's splendour, was an old enemy of Percy's the harbourer for the Staghounds, who was out in search of a stag for a meet in the area the following day.

I was late out the next morning and decided to walk in an area that Percy was likely to pass on his route home should he be pursued. My route took me up through a wooded valley until I emerged out into an open moorland coombe that fell steeply from the high moor. This was my chosen place of wait and settling in amongst a patch of gorse, I reached for my binoculars to scan up the coombe. It was not long before I discovered I was not alone. I could see the tips of antlers which called for a short careful stalk to investigate. The wind was perfectly in my favour, blowing off the moor and down the coombe. The stag had little chance of detecting my approach. Eventually I had crawled to within thirty yards and could get a clear view of him. To my amazement, it turned out to be Percy, apparently alone though perhaps he had company in the bracken. I made a careful but hasty retreat. Percy had clearly left his hinds unattended, perhaps he had read the hunting appointments in the paper or rather sensed danger and slipped quietly away to lie alone in this coombe where I had chanced upon him. I prepared myself for a long wait, determined to stay with him all day to see if he had done enough to save himself.

The time passed, apart from the sight of a few mounted hunt followers in the distance making their way to the meet, everything so far remained peaceful. Percy occasionally shook his head at the torment of flies or was momentarily alerted to the sound of hunters and hounds away over the hill. It was now eleven o'clock and the huntsman would be selecting his tufters for the search for Percy. The next thing I heard was the huntsman's horn encouraging his hounds and then a burst of music as they put up a deer. No doubt it was not suitable for I could still see Percy, the master of the district, lying tightly across the coombe. After a while the cry of the hounds became louder and clearer, then suddenly a spring stag broke the skyline. I wished him away for if the tufters were on his line he was leading them right to Percy. The young stag wasted no time in negotiating the steep deer track off the moor, crossed the coombe and passed below Percy and raced down past me with a slight flinch as he caught my scent but he was not stopping for anything.

There was a moment's grace before hounds broke the skyline in full cry. The leading hound was dropping into the coombe. Percy lay tight for as long as he dared then suddenly he sprang to his feet making a hasty retreat down the coombe, following the line of the young stag and seconds in front of the hounds.

From the top of the coombe the leading riders had viewed Percy away and were no doubt wondering how they had so quickly changed to a warrantable stag. The sound of the hounds was now fading away down the wooded valley as the riders galloped down the bridlepath on the edge of the coombe and entered the cover.

There was no question where Percy would be heading, yet when all had settled down I had not the heart or motivation to head home for I was left pondering over an empty lying bed where Percy had minutes before been safely hidden.

It was early in the afternoon when I reached home. The signs were there that the hunt had passed by — the road was marked with the scuffs of many galloping horseshoes. In a short while I heard the sound of a rider walking his horse back up the road. At last it was someone to ask if there had been a kill. The news was that the stag had gone to sea and the hounds had been called off as the stag was seen to be swimming across Porlock Bay towards Hurlestone Point.

I thanked him. So Percy had gone to sea. In the olden days of hunting that would have been the end for him as the master of the hunt paid the princely sum of half a crown to a boatman at Porlock Weir to be out in wait for any stag that went to sea when the hounds were in the vicinity. Times had changed, along with public opinion. With little, if any, hunting activity along the coast, landowners had little incentive to preserve stags and uncontrolled shooting rendered them scarce. Now that the rare last stag like Percy had gone to sea, the hunt was much quicker in calling off the hounds long before they reached the shore.

Beyond Hurlestone Point where Percy was heading was a dangerous stretch of coastline, an area that I knew well from my boyhood adventuring. As soon as I heard the news I set off for the point, the uncertainty of his destiny had got the better of me.

On reaching the pebble ridge beach I paused to scan out to sea. To my amazement I immediately caught sight of a pair of antlers like a ship's mast rising and falling in the waves some half a mile out. Unfortunately the beach was not deserted. Over by the Point there were some fishermen quite oblivious to everything. I wish there had been time to warn them for by now Percy was obviously making a desperate bid to reach the shore before he was taken around the point by the incoming tide. Keeping out of sight, all I could do was watch the outcome. Closer and closer he came, surely they would see him in a minute. To be expected, when one of them caught sight of him, their reaction was ecstatic excitement. Their shouts and commotion turned Percy back out to sea again. He had no choice but to struggle against the force of the tide and attempt to round Hurlestone Point. As he disappeared out of sight he was clearly being swept closer and closer to the rocks where he would stand no chance.

There was little anyone could do now, the fishermen were left with the tallest of fishing tales to take home and I pondering on what to do next. Only at low tide is it possible to get around the Point, other than obtaining a small boat or swimming. The only option was to attempt to climb the cliffs. It would be foolhardy but I was game to try with nothing to aid me but my determination to know Percy's fate. Climbing up over the Point was easy but the descent to the rocky shore far below was somewhat daunting. The flow of adrenalin seemed to anaesthetise any of my fears, until after a while I was edging my way down closer and closer to the sound and sight of the waves pounding the rocky shore. I managed to reach a large rock not yet covered by the tide and I sat exhausted and recovering from the descent. There seemed little hope for Percy and no sign of him as I scanned despairingly with my binoculars. I knew I could not afford to stay long; the tide was rising rapidly and threatening to cut off the rock I was sitting on. Soaked from the spray of the breaking waves, I took a last long hard look. Then something floating in the sea took my notice. It was either a large piece of driftwood or it was the drowned body of Percy.

I studied it hard as it was being washed ashore. Eventually I could see that it had hair upon it and my worst fears were realised — it was Percy. I felt shocked and saddened and somewhat amazed at the incredible chance in a million that the body was being carried to the exact rocky area that I was standing on. The last few vital feet then I grasped an antler. Having taken his antlers I eventually had to leave Percy to his watery grave in this inaccessible place. It was somewhat ironic that Hurlestone Point, where Percy met his sad end, was in clear view from his favourite lying bed in the paddock next to my cottage. He might have planned it all.

Percy's final resting place.

CONCLUSION

This personal study of the deer of Exmoor was completed in 1989. Left on hold for ten years until now when 1998 sees its publication. In that time much has happened. At the 1990 A.G.M. of The National Trust a resolution was proposed by Mrs D Cronin and Mrs D Wilson of the Devon and Somerset Residents Association for Deer Protection to prohibit the hunting of deer with hounds on certain National Trust land on Exmoor and the Quantocks.

The resolution was passed but the Trust's council reiterated its policy that ethical and moral arguments for and against hunting should be decided by Parliament. It also decided to set up a working party, under Professor RJG Savage, on the conservation and management of Red deer on the Quantocks and on Exmoor, including the various implications of a ban on hunting. The working party noted that the terms of reference did not request any investigations of ethical or moral issues.

In March 1993 the working party reported and made a series of recommendations to provide effective deer management, combined with a study of the possible need for legislation in England and Wales to assist in overall deer management.

At the 1993 A.G.M. a resolution (resolution 6) urged the council to continue to implement Trust policy in relation to wildlife conservation, in accordance with the statutory purposes of the Trust and the best interests of its work, whilst leaving the ethical or moral considerations to be determined by Parliament. This was passed by 100,723 votes to 29,722. But at the same meeting another resolution (resolution 7), proposed by Lord Soper, sought to set up a balanced working party on deer hunting, to examine issues relating to cruelty and animal welfare not addressed in the Savage report. This resolution could not be voted on in 1993 because of a High Court ruling that the agenda document and proxy voting form had not been prepared in such a way as to avoid any real risk of confusion to members voting on the resolution .

On the 16th July 1994, the Trust held both the adjourned 1993 Annual General Meeting and an Extraordinary General Meeting. At the A.A.G.M the resolution to set up a balanced working party on deer hunting (resolution 7), was passed by 111,606 votes to 94,733. At the E.G.M. a resolution on deer hunting was proposed, basically similar to the 1993 resolution 7, but with some variations. In particular, that the balanced working party should be led by an independent chairman. This was passed by 114,837 votes to 99,607. It was as a result of its consideration of this E.G.M. resolution that the council unanimously agreed in April 1995 to invite Professor Bateson F.R.S., to conduct a scientific study into suffering as a welfare factor in Red deer on Exmoor and the Quantocks. The terms of reference were as follows:-

"To study suffering as a welfare factor in the management of Red deer on National Trust properties on Exmoor and the Quantocks, having regard, inter alia, to the scientific evidence on stress induced in deer by hunting with hounds and by other culling methods, animal welfare legislation, and the likely effects, in so far as they can be estimated, of a hunting ban on suffering among deer".

In 1997 Professor Bateson's study was complete and after the council had considered the results of his report, hunting deer with hounds on all National Trust property, where possible, was banned by the National Trust council. The Forestry Commission soon followed.

At the same time, a Private Member's Bill was brought up in parliament by the Labour MP Michael Foster, to outlaw the hunting of wild animals with dogs. A free vote in Parliament saw a majority of 260 MPs in favour of the Bill, but so far it has not been given enough parliamentary time to enable it to become law.

The 1990's also saw the deer of Exmoor again the subject of another scientific study, looking into their ranging behaviour, habitat use and the impact of deer in oak woods and heather moor. This three year study was conducted by Dr Jochen Langbein and was sponsored by most parties with an interest in the deer. When the study was produced the media reports homed in on one of Langbein's findings, that there were probably more deer in the West Country now than for 500 years and that they were contributing to damage to Exmoor woodlands. Dr Langbein's report is impressive in its attention to detail.

Concerning estimation of numbers we are in close agreement. Over balance of the sexes, Langbein found 2.5-1 in favour of females, which was far higher and more serious than I found it to be. Not covered in his objectives was a study of the quality of the herds. It is my opinion that of the imbalance of the sexes, the most serious shortage is of large, mature stags with good heads of antlers.

This shortage can also be missed on large scale annual deer counts which are organised in the West Country. The Quantock Hill area is covered by the "Quantock Deer Management & Conservation Group", and for Exmoor the "Exmoor and District Deer Management Society". When counting, volunteers list male deer only into two categories, Pricket or Stag. So if there was not even one three a-top stag, say, on the Quantocks, the organised count would not pick this up and the situation could appear healthy, but with the majority of the stags young and immature

Dr Langbein and myself are both in agreement over the need for closer management of the deer herds. He also came up against the secrecy of the deer shooting fraternity. He spoke of "no reliable information. Too great a proportion of landowners or those holding the shooting rights were unwilling to disclose information on culls taken to provide good estimations of actual off-take". Dr Langbein approached well over 50 different people who were known to undertake some culling of Red deer, with the request to provide (in confidence) records of Red deer culls taken by them. For various reasons only 14 stalkers and some of the hunts provided detailed information.

Since the National Trust ban on deer hunting on its land, reports of massive recent slaughters of deer on private land have been rife, especially on the Quantock Hills, where deer hunting has been worst affected. In November 1997 one local paper featured an article which had the headline "Somerset's Stags Paying Price For Trust Hunting Ban", and showed a picture of 30-40 stags' heads and spoke of unconfirmed reports that half of the Quantocks stags had been shot by private landowners and sent profitably to local game dealers.

Conservationists said it would not be possible to gauge the extent of the killings until the spring census of the Quantock herd was carried out in March, but they feared talk of the heavy cull may be true.

The West Country of England is a wonderful and unique part of our English heritage and the wild Red deer are an integral part of its beauty. The deer are facing unprecedented pressures and are caught up in a battle of human conflicts. Hunting has preserved Red deer for centuries in the West Country and as its hold over the deer is gradually eroded, so the deer pay the price. With the ever increasing likelihood of the abolition of blood sports without protective legislation for the deer of Exmoor, then they are sure to suffer their most significant decline this century

Fine growing stag out in the open.

Big stag being hunted, Exe Valley 1985.

At Hawkcombe Head, looking towards Selworthy.

Two fine Porlock stags in winter.

Predicting the extent of this certain catastrophe is open to debate and though it will certainly be a disaster for the deer, it is unlikely that it will lead to complete extinction, as blood sports supporters so often warn us

Over the issue of low numbers of deer on Exmoor and the Quantocks, Dr Langbein writes "the question of minimum viable populations on Exmoor and the Quantocks does not really arise, as these sub-populations are part of a much wider 'population', stretching well into Devon and Cornwall, as well as Somerset. Occasional influx of animals from other areas would seem likely to recolonise the area even if populations on Exmoor and the Quantock Hills themselves were ever to fall to negligible levels."

I would suggest that if the main concentrations of Red deer in the West Country, which are known to centre on Exmoor and the Quantock Hills, which Dr Langbein describes as the sub-population of a main population, are so seriously decimated then for the same reasons, it is likely that the main population will have suffered the same fate.

In my opinion, numbers of Red deer that are found living in Devon and Cornwall and beyond the Quantock Hills in other parts of Somerset are very negligible and I question the likelihood of Dr Langbein's theory. Indeed, even if a recolonisation was seen after a disaster, what hope would a few returning deer have of thriving and increasing, if the playing field was the same.

Conservationists are often reminded by the blood sports lobby of what happened to the Red deer during the mid 18th century when stag hunting on Exmoor failed and with it deer numbers sunk to low levels. The Exmoor of today is a very different place, a "National Park" and despite most of the land remaining in private ownership, there is good reason today to be very optimistic over the chances of a number of wild Red deer being around for a very long time. The National Park Authority itself owns around 6.8% of the land, a further 10% is under the control of the National Trust another large landowner is the League Against Cruel Sports. None of these landowners would ever adopt a policy of complete eradication of deer.

76.8% of Exmoor remains in private ownership, of which there are likely to be many who would be sympathetic to the deer, even without hunting. Another significant sanctuary will be Exmoor's wonderful wild and inaccessible coastline. The most likely outcome of a deer hunting ban in Parliament, without legislation passed to assist in management and preservation of this wild animal, is a few fragmented pockets of wild Red deer with a low number of stags. They may well survive well into the next century and beyond thanks to a few friends, but mainly due to inaccessible habitat coupled with the deer's cunning powers of survival against all the odds and under intense pressure.

In an ideal world it would be nice to read a naturalist's report on the wild Red deer of Exmoor in, say, 2050. I hope it might read something like this

"Despite the abolition of hunting deer with hounds, a sound working system of deer management and conservation was put in place to protect the wild Red deer in the West Country. The deer on Exmoor are today highly regarded as an asset to the Park and have been given lawful wildlife status. Long gone are the days when they could be treated as a pest. Immediately after the abolition of deer hunting the Government set up a "Red Deer Commission", with its base on Exmoor and working with the National Park Authority. To qualify for conservation (E.S.A.) grants, farmers and landowners have to co-operate and adhere to the Commission. Generous extra grants are paid out to compensate for deer damage.

All culling, when necessary, is carried out by "only" Commission appointed stalkers, who each have their own areas to control. Each stalker is highly trained and uses a trained dog to, on the rare occasion, follow up a wounded deer. Licences for possession of rifles are not issued to any individual or landowner, who must as part of the scheme, only allow Commission appointed stalkers on their land. Shotgun licences are granted for pest control and game shooting, but it is a serious offence to use the shotgun on deer. A new-set aside grant for woodlands was implemented on Exmoor to preserve undisturbed woodland covers for deer and wildlife and curtail the massive increase in commercial pheasant shooting.

The commission is still partly funded from Government grants, but is striving to be self-sufficient through the "Red Deer Fund". Money is raised in various ways including tourism, stalking, venison sales, lottery grants and much fund raising by the local community, proud of their wildlife. The Commission have their own sanctuary area in the Exe Valley, which is also a Visitor Centre and Deer Interpretation Centre. Safaris around the sanctuary, as well as around Exmoor, led by National Park rangers, benefit the Red Deer

On Lucott Moor.

Stags out on the forest.

The heads of the valley.

Afternoon stroll.

Fund. Some of the culling is let to the paying gun who has to pass a regular, rigorous stalking proficiency test and must be led by a Commission appointed stalker. All revenue from stalking benefits the deer through the Red Deer Fund.

The Commission-appointed stalkers know their areas intimately and the deer situation. Each regularly reports to the Commission on numbers and the cull is set by the commission with the issue of official tags for hinds and for stags. The number one aim is to maintain a high quality herd and an even balance of the sexes. As well as setting the cull, the Commission also manages the granting of compensatory payments to farmers for deer damage to crops and hedges. All culled deer from Exmoor have to be sent with their official cull tag to the Red Deer Commission's central hanging and dressing point at Exford. Some carcasses are sold on to game dealers, some venison can be distributed to farmers and landowners as part of their compensation and there is also a good local market for Exmoor venison. Today one can eat venison from Exmoor in the knowledge that it is the harvest from a sound working management and conservation system for the wild Red deer and that all profits from venison benefit the species.

Such is the merest sketch of a system that has saved this animal when a few years ago its future was in doubt. It is a cold January day in 2050 and I am standing on the heather clad slopes of Mill Hill on Exmoor, watching a wintering bunch of Exmoor stags. There are forty or more of them and I can only marvel at their array of antlers, a moving forest, as they make their way towards a feeding point run by the Red Deer Commission. The roots they are given only, in winter, help them through this leanest of times".

I sincerely hope that such a system is put in place. It could be put in place now and staghunting for as long as it remains a legal method of killing an animal, could be incorporated into the scheme, and bring hunting and shooting back in harmony again.

Surely then the future for the wild Red deer of Exmoor would be assured and there would not only be plenty of fine old Exmoor stags with Brow, Bay and Trey, carrying all the rights on their heads, and so, not before time, being given all the rights to a secure future, for they were here first.

The End